Make Life Good

"*Make Life Good* is a simple little book that takes on big-world and life-changing issues. I will be a better man for having invested the time to read Randy's book. I encourage you to do the same."

—**Bruce Scott**, SVP, Business Development of Westfall Gold

"*Make Life Good* poses the poignant question, "Why do you do what you do?" This single question will take us on a journey beyond our wildest imagination. A journey that gives life to us and everyone we encounter."

—**Bill Williams**, past president of National Christian Foundation and past president of Generous Giving

"In a society where success is too often equated with comfort, it's easy to lose sight of a purposeful life. *Make Life Good* paints a beautiful picture of what a life with purpose looks like and emblazons a map on each reader's heart, showing them how to get there."

—**James Whitford**, founder and CEO of True Charity Initiative

"*Make Life Good* is a powerful reminder that proper stewardship ensures the legacy of the donor and the mission of the organization are aligned to provide an impactful pathway to change lives together."

—**Captain Paul Ryerson**, Commanding Officer of The Salvation Army of Gwinnett County, GA

"*Make Life Good* gets to the 'why,' which is so much more important than the 'how' or the 'what.' 'Why' is different for everyone, but it is important for non-profits to understand that it's pivotal in the art of successfully raising money. 'What' you do and 'how' you do it are easy to explain. 'Why' takes some work, and Randy's book will help you get there."

—**Tom Ralser**, Principal of Convergent Nonprofit Solutions and author of *Asking Rights: Why Some Nonprofits Get Funded (and some don't)*

"As the principles of a fruitful and fulfilling life are revealed in *Make Life Good*, your vision of what a life of true significance means will begin to take shape, and you will discover that there is 'something more' than mere success. A rewarding journey awaits!"

—**Dr. Beverly Upton Williams**, CEO of Haggai International

"There is a yearning for eternity, meaning, and purpose placed within each of us as an invitation to a greater story. Randy's parable will spark an explosion of questions and discovery that may change the way you work and inspire you to live a legacy!"

—**Mike Sharrow**, CEO of C12 Business Forums

"*Make Life Good* is far better than good; it's revelational! I urge you to make your life better by reading and putting into practice the truths found in these pages."

—**Bruce Deel,** founder and CEO of City of Refuge, Inc.

"Every once in a while a book comes along that I consider a 'must read.' *Make Life Good* is such a book! In these pages you will find life-transforming principles wrapped up in an engaging storyline that is certain to make you rethink issues such as meaning, purpose, and generosity."

—**Daryl Heald**, founder of Generosity Path and
former Director of Generosity, The Maclellan Foundation

"Our unique journeys through life are like time capsules wrapped in the cloak of eras passed and, ideally, for the future benefit of all who follow behind us. In *Make Life Good*, protagonist Joe walks us through a crisis of belief that will feel familiar to many. We are challenged to 'think globally and act locally' as we intentionally pack our capsules with things that matter, sacrifices that shape the world around us, and actions that impact eternity.

—**John Heerema**, CEO of Biglife International Inc.

"I heartily recommend reading *Make Life Good* if you want to move beyond a 'stuck' worldview to understand the wonderful providences of God's will for each of us."

—**Jimmy Dorrell**, founder of Mission Waco | Mission World and Church Under the Bridge

"A parable is a powerful way to communicate a message. This one in particular is packed with thought-provoking questions and principles that will transform you from the inside out. You'll want to read *Make Life Good* and then pass it along so that others will be impacted by its message."

—**Tim Elmore**, founder of Growing Leaders and author of *A New Kind of Diversity*

"*Make Life Good* exposes the core of what every person desires in their deepest being . . . to have a good life that makes an impact and leaves a lasting legacy."

—**Ike Reighard**, President and CEO of MUST Ministries

"*Make Life Good* reminds us that true success and fulfillment come not just from financial success, but from living a life of purpose and meaning. This is your treasure map to find sustaining joy in life!"

—**Rich DeAugustinis**, retired Coca-Cola Executive and Non-Profit Leader

"Randy's well-told story is a catalyst of self-reflection that challenges and guides each reader to take the steps necessary to leave a lasting legacy of good."

—**Terry Johnson**, Chief Revenue and Strategy Officer of Generational Group

"The opening question in Chapter 1 is worth the price of *Make Life Good*. It's a bit unsettling, thought-provoking, and challenging. The rest of the book will inspire you to 'make life good.'"

—**Jeff Henderson**, founder of The FOR Company and author of *What to Do Next*

"If you're looking for a way to impact your world for the good, you just found it. *Make Life Good* will transform the way you view and relate to your world."

—**David L. Hancock**, Advisory Board Member of Habitat for Humanity

"Few books capture the heart, the mind, and the will to make a difference. *Make Life Good* does and it will change the way you see the world — for good!"

—**Cheryl Bachelder**, former CEO of Popeyes Louisiana Kitchen, Inc., author of *Dare to Serve*, and board member of WorkMatters Ministry

"*Make Life Good* weaves together a beautiful story of what really matters, and how we each can make a difference. Dr. Ross both challenges and encourages us to understand and experience the fact that true happiness isn't something that can be achieved, but is a natural byproduct of doing good for others."

—**Neal Joseph**, Co-Founder & Managing Partner of Mission:Leadership

"Having served thousands of people facing homelessness, I know firsthand that engaging in meeting needs around you is transformational. If you read *Make Life Good* with an open mind and heart, it could change your life forever!"

—**Jim Reese**, former president & CEO of Atlanta Mission

"Profound questions create cognitive dissonance and *Make Life Good* is filled with them. 'Why do you do what you do?' 'Is it fulfilling?' 'Is it meaningful?' If you want to change the trajectory of your life and the lives of those around you, read Dr. Randy's book … and then give a copy to someone you care about."

—**Dr. Thomas Lutz**, Chair of Convene and author of
Equipping Christians for Kingdom Purpose in Their Work

"Each one of us has been entrusted with a God-given responsibility to make the world a better place. *Make Life Good* serves as a reminder that as individuals and organizations, we can do that if we are willing to step outside of ourselves and recognize God's prompting, responding to the world around us with love and compassion."

> —**Dr. Bob Page**, Chief of Chaplains at Marketplace Chaplains
> and Chaplain, Brigadier General, USAF (Retired)

"As a leader committed to personal and professional growth, I wholeheartedly endorse *Make Life Good*. Dr. Randy Ross' insights provide a refreshing perspective on success, encouraging readers to build a life that truly matters.

> —**Mark Cole**, CEO of Maxwell Leadership

"Inspirational read for all those looking to find their true purpose in life."

> —**Jay and Tracy Arntzen**, founders of SSM Ministry

"We make a living by what we get.
We make a life by what we give."
—Winston Churchill

"The meaning of life is to find your gift.
The purpose of life is to give it away."
—Pablo Picasso

"Give and it will be given to you. A good portion—
packed down, firmly shaken, and overflowing—
will fall into your lap. The portion you give will
determine the portion you receive in return."
—The NIV Bible, Luke 6:38

You've Made a
Good Living, Now...

MAKE
LIFE
GOOD

A Soul-Stirring Parable
About What Really Matters

DR. RANDY ROSS

NEW YORK

LONDON • NASHVILLE • MELBOURNE • VANCOUVER

Make Life Good

A Soul-Stirring Parable About What Really Matters

Published in New York, New York, by Morgan James Publishing. Morgan James is a trademark of Morgan James, LLC. www.MorganJamesPublishing.com

Proudly distributed by Publishers Group West®

Scripture taken from the Holy Bible, New International Version®, NIV®. Copyright © 1973, 1978, 1984, 2011 by Biblica, Inc.™. Used by permission of Zondervan. All rights reserved worldwide. www.zondervan.com The "NIV" and "New International Version" are trademarks registered in the United States Patent and Trademark Office by Biblica, Inc.™

Illustrations by Jim Howell. Editing by Kay Acton.

Morgan James BOGO™

A **FREE** ebook edition is available for you or a friend with the purchase of this print book.

CLEARLY SIGN YOUR NAME ABOVE

Instructions to claim your free ebook edition:
1. Visit MorganJamesBOGO.com
2. Sign your name CLEARLY in the space above
3. Complete the form and submit a photo of this entire page
4. You or your friend can download the ebook to your preferred device

ISBN 9781636983592 paperback
ISBN 9781636983608 ebook
Library of Congress Control Number: 2023948952

Cover Design by:
FormattedBooks
www.formattedbooks.com

Interior Design by:
FormattedBooks
www.formattedbooks.com

Morgan James is a proud partner of Habitat for Humanity Peninsula and Greater Williamsburg. Partners in building since 2006.

Get involved today! Visit: www.morgan-james-publishing.com/giving-back

CONTENTS

FOREWORD

The late theologian and author Frederick Buechner articulated the goals of both life and work well when he said, "Your vocation in life is where your greatest joy meets the world's greatest need." I was reminded of that wise instruction as I read *Make Life Good*. We should neither seek a self-centered vocation that brings no value to the world nor labor joylessly for a worthy cause that gives us no personal satisfaction.

Identifying your greatest joy and giftedness and then arranging your life to serve others is the challenge we all face. That type of contribution is a focus of the organization that I'm privileged to lead, Compassion International, where we strive to see children released from poverty in Jesus' name. Given that important mission, thoughts about how to live a good and abundant life as we meet the needs of others are often at the forefront of my mind. So I was deeply honored when Randy invited me to offer this small contribution to his book that champions a similar outcome for us all.

I've had the privilege of leading as a CEO for more than 30 years, at two wonderful and high-performing cause-driven organizations. And in both of those environments, it's been a joy to link arms with thousands of passionate people as they employ their unique giftedness and expertise in service to a meaningful cause. And across those many years of leadership, I've had a front-row seat in witnessing the richness of vocations dedicated to life-transforming efforts.

However, a full-time role in the social sector was not what I initially envisioned for my life. I trained to be an engineer like my dad and always thought I'd follow in his footsteps of being a successful professional who was passionate about philanthropy. There's great value in that path as well. The ministry I lead simply could not exist without the generosity of caring supporters who are deeply committed to helping the less fortunate and who joyfully give of themselves to lift others up. I regularly encounter people from all walks of life who approach their work as a means of not only providing for their own families but also serving society and helping to change the world for the better, even if that means changing the world of just one person.

Regardless of your vocation, I do hope you are blessed with a life path that blends the work you most need to do with the work the world most needs to have done. Joy and fulfillment are found and a good life is lived when those dynamics come together to make a difference that only you can make.

—**Santiago "Jimmy" Mellado**
President and CEO
of Compassion International

INTRODUCTION

We are the world.

On January 28, 1985, some of the most famous artists in the music industry gathered to record a benefit single for African famine relief. The single was written by Michael Jackson and Lionel Richie in less than seven weeks and completed just one night before the recording session. The song that captured the attention and imagination of the world was produced by Quincy Jones and Michael Omartian. And it was the clarion call of activist Harry Belafonte, along with fundraiser Ken Kragen, that brought the vision to reality.

The charity single sold more than 20 million copies and ignited a firestorm of support for a cause that affected our global community. For many, it was the first time they had been captivated by concerns beyond their own borders. It spawned a movement and united a generation to consider what could be done if they simply joined hands to do good. The message of "We Are the World" was indelibly imprinted on our collective consciousness, reminding us that we—you and me—can make a brighter day for others when we start giving.

1

THE QUESTION

"Why do you do what you do?"

The question jarred him back into the moment. "Excuse me?"

"Why do you do what you do?" The weather-worn man asked the question so casually it was easy to dismiss.

"Don't you mean, what do I do?"

"No. What you do is far less important than why you do it," he said. Then he repeated the question, "*Why* do you do what you do?"

It was a simple, yet stunning, query.

And a strange one, too, coming from a … homeless man? Joe had seen him at this intersection several times before, walking between the cars with his crumpled cardboard sign. Joe looked down at his sign again to confirm what was written on it. In big black letters that had obviously been hand-scrawled, it read, "Need Help?"

Wait, what? Joe thought. That wasn't what he remembered being on the sign. Or maybe he just hadn't really paid much attention before.

The light at this particular intersection was an annoyance that had frequently elongated his trip home from work. As he sat at this spot, his mind usually raced, reflecting upon the conversations that had consumed his day. He was typically oblivious to many details as he sped through life. But today was different. Today his thoughts ran deeper. He had been contemplating whether there might be a deeper meaning to life than the rat race that had defined his existence. For some reason, Joe decided to roll down his window as the man with the long beard and scraggly appearance walked his way.

A ten-dollar bill was sitting in the cup holder. Joe didn't typically give homeless beggars the time of day, but today he felt more generous than usual. After all, he had just received a significant promotion and raise at work. Maybe this was his way of expressing gratitude to the universe in the hopes that the universe would continue to be good to him. At the very least, he thought, the small gift might keep the dirty man away from his new blue Mercedes-Benz EQS 450, with its vanity plate that read, "STYLING."

"So?"

"So what?"

"You haven't answered my question." His statement was pointed, yet his tone was strangely soothing.

"Why do I do what I do? I don't know. It's what I studied in college. It's what I do to support my family. It's where life has taken me, I suppose."

"Is it fulfilling?"

It was another odd question, and there was no time to respond. The light was now green and the impatient driver in the car behind him was honking. Joe quickly handed the man the ten-dollar bill and mumbled something about not wasting it on booze. Then he accelerated through the intersection and drove home.

2

DISTRACTED

After dinner Joe helped his wife, Kathy, clean the kitchen and retreated to the family room. He turned on the television and scrolled through the channels until he found the game he wanted to watch. It was well into the first quarter, with the score tied. He'd been looking forward to watching the game all day. Although he had a vested interest in the outcome, he found it hard to focus on the game. He was distracted, thinking about the conversation earlier with the homeless man.

"Is it fulfilling?" Those words echoed in his head like rolling thunder in a canyon.

He thought through how he might respond, should he see the vagabond again. Of course, his job was fulfilling! He had the title he had always wanted and the compensation package to back it up. His family was well cared for, and his son's and daughter's college tuition accounts fully funded. What more could he possibly want?

The rest of the evening his thoughts bounced back and forth between the game and his imagined response to the nagging question.

That night, something kept nudging him out of a sound sleep. Several times he thought he had heard movement in the house. But each time he awakened, the noises stopped.

When he started to drift back to sleep, he found himself reliving the question: "Is it fulfilling?" In that foggy zone between starlight and slumber, the homeless man wandered into his dreams. He could smell his musty clothes and sense the soothing tone of his voice. But what haunted him most were the words on his sign: "Need Help?" He could have sworn from previous sightings that it read, "Need Help!"

The rising sun rudely interrupted his shallow slumber. Joe's morning routine redirected his attention as he prepared for the day. Once in his car, he wondered if he would see the man on his way to work. But as he approached the intersection, there was no sign of the stranger. For a moment he was disappointed. He wouldn't be able to provide his well-thought-out answer to the probing question, at least for now.

3

AT THE OFFICE

Joe parked his car in his reserved space and entered the building. Once on the 14th floor, he greeted everyone as he usually did on his way to his corner office. After unpacking his briefcase, he went to the break room for coffee.

As he poured his cup of java, he glanced at the corkboard that hung on the wall above the serving station. In the middle of the board, four red thumbtacks secured a single sheet of paper. On the sheet was a single word. Written in bold red letters was the question "Why?"

He had never seen it before. There was no indication as to who put it there and no explanation of its meaning. But it immediately took him back to his encounter the day before with the vagabond.

"Why do you do what you do?" He stood there staring at the inquiry.

He fell into this line of work right out of college. It seemed like a logical transition after earning his degree. The organization that recruited him had offered a significant amount of money, considering his rookie status. Certainly, more than any of the other groups that had expressed interest. For Joe, it was a no-brainer. He jumped at the opportunity to make that kind of "bank" straight out of school.

The job didn't turn out to be everything that he had hoped it would be, but it did have its perks. In just a few years a company car dulled the pain of the long hours that took him away from family dinners, ball games, and recitals. A hefty spending account allowed him to distract himself and entertain clients while away on business trips in distant cities. And his salary package and vacation time afforded him and his family the opportunity to travel to exotic destinations.

He worked hard and was highly respected. He had everything he thought he wanted. So how could such a simple question haunt him so as he roamed the shadows of his mind in search of an answer? He was lost in his thoughts when Kevin entered the break room.

Joe always enjoyed chatting with Kevin, a coworker from Human Resources, whenever they bumped into each other. Joe respected Kevin and looked up to him as somewhat of a corporate big brother, since he was a little further along in his career. Bright and successful, he had a beautiful wife and three kids. But that's about all Joe knew about Kevin. Most of their conversations centered around work. Rarely did they ever venture into the realm of personal matters.

"Enjoying the trip?" Kevin's voice interrupted his contemplation.

"What?"

"Looked like you were somewhere over the rainbow. Welcome back!"

"You caught me deep in thought—which is rare!" Joe quipped, trying to brush off the awkwardness of the moment.

"You were deep all right. Deep in something. Did you bring Dorothy back with you?" Kevin smirked, his dry sense of humor shining through.

"No. She's still trying to find the Wizard," Joe retorted.

Kevin made himself at home at the coffee station as Joe slowly walked toward the door.

But almost instinctively he turned back to Kevin and asked, "Hey, do you know who put that 'Why?' sign up there on the board?" Joe asked.

"That 'Why?' sign? Well yes, I do. Why?"

"Cute," Joe sighed. "Do you know who put it there?"

"I did." Kevin admitted.

"*Why?*"

"Exactly!"

"Exactly what?"

"No, why?"

"OK, this is beginning to sound like an old Abbot and Costello routine. What made you put up that sign?" Joe asked.

"Not what, but *Why*," Kevin said jokingly. "Alright, alright— enough of the comedy shtick. The reason I put it there is because I think it's a good question to ask from time to time."

It's easy sometimes to get lost wandering through life and going through the motions without any real meaning or passion.

"What do you mean?" Joe started retracing his steps back toward Kevin.

"Well, it's easy sometimes to get lost wandering through life and going through the motions without any real meaning or passion. That question helps me sharpen my focus by staying grounded in my purpose."

"Staying grounded in your purpose? What the heck does that mean?"

"Ah, Grasshopper, if you really want to know, then pull up a chair and sit at the feet of your sensei." There was a twinkle in Kevin's eyes as he said it half-jokingly. It was the other half that drew Joe in.

Joe pulled up a chair and sat at the table. After adding creamer to his coffee, Kevin joined him.

4

THE CONVERSATION

Joe had always maintained a strict separation between his personal and professional lives. He felt it was better that way. If he ever had a challenge on the home front, he was able to effectively mask it so no one in the office would know. He was a master of keeping his image untarnished in the business. To do otherwise, he felt, would not serve him well.

However, his encounter with the homeless man had taken him down a mental rabbit hole that left him confused and curious. He had found himself wrestling with questions he could not easily answer. That struggle had made him cautiously vulnerable.

"Alright, what do you want to know?" Kevin asked.

"Grounded in your purpose? What exactly does that mean?"

"Well, Joe, what would you say is your purpose in life?"

After reflecting momentarily, Joe responded, "I don't know. I suppose to provide the very best for my family and to enjoy life."

"And then what?" Kevin leaned in.

"And then die! What do you mean, 'And then what?'"

"What do you want to be known for? What kind of legacy do you want to leave? What dent do you want to make in the universe? If all you do is breathe this air and leave things the same way you found them when you arrived on this planet, then what's the point?"

"The point," Joe quipped, "would be that I worked hard and took care of my family. That I set my kids up for success, by giving them experiences and resources I never had. That I enjoyed life and did my best. That I fulfilled most of my dreams. I would say that's a pretty darn good life." Joe leaned back in his chair and folded his arms as if to justify his answer.

What do you want to be known for? What kind of legacy do you want to leave?

"That it would," Kevin acknowledged. "But would it be meaningful? Would it be satisfying? Would it make a real difference in the world?"

"For me and my family it would!" Joe asserted.

"It would, indeed," Kevin affirmed. "And that may be enough. But what if you could do something that went beyond yourself and your inner circle? What if you were able to be a part of something much larger? What if you were able to make a real difference in the world? What if you were literally able to change the world for good?"

Your life is a gift to the world. But a life wrapped up in itself makes a very small package.

Joe didn't know where this line of questioning was going. His brow furrowed and his eyes narrowed a bit. "Come on, Kevin, that's the kind of big talk of polished politicians and pipe dreamers. Changing the world is a mighty big order, don't you think? I'm not sure anyone can 'make a dent in the universe,' unless you're Steve Jobs. And frankly I don't like wearing black crewneck shirts!"

"I'm not too keen on black shirts myself," Kevin admitted. "But here's the thing. Your life is a gift to the world. But a life wrapped up in itself makes a very small package. There's a lot to be gained by looking beyond your immediate surroundings and exploring ways in which you might be able to help others."

"Like giving to a food drive or clothing to a homeless shelter?" Joe asked.

"Sure, that's certainly a start. But has that really cost you anything? Don't get me wrong, doing good is doing good. But what I've found to be true is that to really be meaningful, an act of charity must actually cost you something. To be truly charitable, it must also be sacrificial."

Joe squirmed nervously in his chair with his arms still folded. He had often given out of convenience, but he was pretty sure he'd never given on a level that could in any way be classified as sacrificial.

His mind wandered to the time his wife had coerced him into joining the family in serving a Thanksgiving meal at a shelter for women who were victims of domestic violence. It was the first time he had become personally involved in meeting the needs of others. It warmed his heart to watch the women and their children enjoy the holiday celebration. But he had to admit that even that investment of time and energy didn't come close to bordering on sacrificial.

Kevin took a long, slow sip of his coffee. Then he continued, "For life to be purposeful, I've discovered that I need to be a part of something bigger than myself. It's not enough just to seek to be my best. I have to create value for others. Value that they could not have created for themselves."

"Alright, I'm listening," Joe said.

"Hey, do you remember the name Abraham Maslow from your Psychology 101 class in college?"

"Vaguely," Joe replied. "Wasn't he known for his *Hierarchy of Needs*?"

"Exactly!" Kevin affirmed, with a smile.

5

THE PYRAMID

"Maslow's *Hierarchy of Needs* was a five-tier pyramid," Kevin began.

He grabbed a napkin lying nearby and began to draw as he continued.

"It was an attempt to explain the motivational factors behind human behavior. On the lowest level were basic *Physiological Needs*, like food, shelter, and clothing. The second tier was *Safety*, or the need for a sense of security. The third level was *Love and Belonging*, which comes from finding connection in a community. Next was *Esteem Needs*, or having a sense of self-worth. And do you remember what the fifth and final tier was called?"

"Hmm," he pondered momentarily. "Nope, not a clue. I likely slept in and missed that class," Joe offered in jest.

"You weren't the only one! Most people don't remember. Maslow labeled the top tier *Self-Actualization,* which simply means becoming all you're destined to be. Doing well for yourself and taking care of yourself. Kinda like how you described your purpose: working hard to see your dreams fulfilled and enjoying life," Kevin stated.

"So, then, that's as good as it gets, right? It's the top tier!" Joe declared.

"Well, not exactly. You see, late in life good-old Abe came to a deeper level of understanding about what drives human behavior and brings fulfillment to life. A friend of his encouraged him to reconsider his motivational theory. He questioned whether or not *Self-Actualization* should actually be the pinnacle of the pyramid.

> *Suppose someone truly fulfills their potential and becomes all they were meant to be. So what? What has that person done to improve the human condition?*

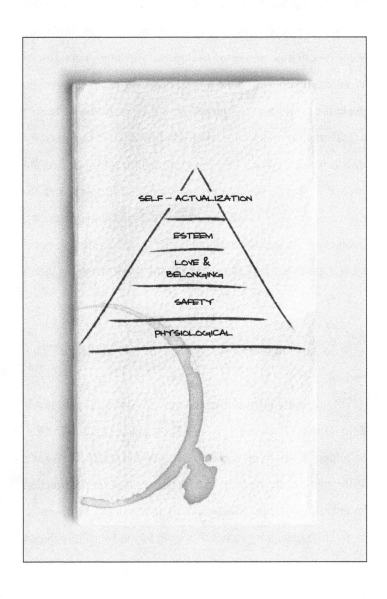

Here was his logic. Suppose someone truly fulfills their potential and becomes all they were meant to be. So what? What has that person done to improve the human condition? What has that person done to give back? How has that person made the world a better place? And if a person never makes a difference in the world, what was the point of that person's life? It would've been nothing more than a self-absorbed existence, focused entirely upon personal consumption and accomplishments. It wouldn't create much of a legacy. In fact, that person's tombstone might accurately read, 'He was born. He was successful. Then he died.' Pretty uninspiring, wouldn't you say?"

His question hung in the air.

"So how did Maslow respond to the challenge?" Joe probed.

"Eventually he modified the pyramid to include three additional tiers. Between *Esteem Needs* and *Self-Actualization*, he added the tiers of *Cognitive Needs* and *Aesthetic Needs*. More importantly, he added a tier above *Self-Actualization* that he called *Self-Transcendence*. This new top tier represented motivation driven by values that went beyond self. It included connecting with a higher purpose, religious pursuits, and, most notably, service to others."

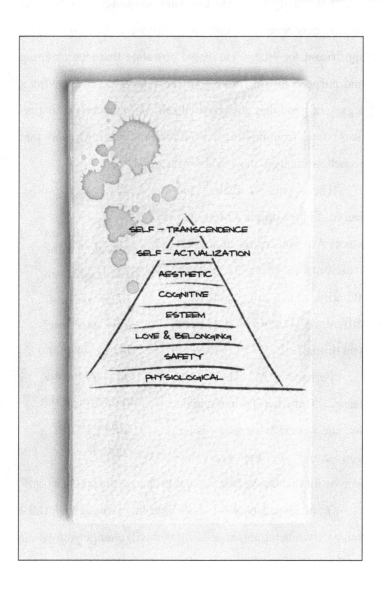

"Essentially what Maslow later suggested was that our earthly existence is not complete until we've done something significant for others. He would postulate that true meaning and purpose in life come from creating value and leaving a legacy of good that goes beyond self. He believed that happiness comes from making a difference and leaving a mark that somehow changes the world for the good."

"There you go again," Joe jeered. "The world is a pretty big place. Are you trying to suggest that someone like you or I can actually make any significant difference? That's a bit bold don't you think?"

"Perhaps it is," Kevin confessed. "But what if you could do for one person what you wished you could do for everyone? Maybe for that one person you could change the whole world!"

What if you could do for one person what you wished you could do for everyone? Maybe for that one person you could change the whole world!

Kevin leaned back to share one more thought: "And I can pretty much guarantee doing that will change your whole world too!"

Joe had never thought of doing good as changing someone else's world. Maybe changing his own little corner of the world was indeed changing the world for good. Maybe it didn't have to be grandiose. Maybe it just meant changing someone's reality and opening a door of opportunity for someone who couldn't open it for themselves. His mind was spinning with possibilities.

> *Happiness comes from making a difference and leaving a mark that somehow changes the world for the good.*

"Maybe you could think about it," Kevin said as he stood up from his chair and made his way to the door. "We can pick it up from here later, if you want to continue the conversation."

Before he could respond, Kevin was out the door and down the hall. The hook had been baited and set. Joe was firmly on the line.

6

THE LIGHT

Joe was about to accelerate through the intersection when the light turned yellow.

Remembering there was a camera mounted on the traffic light pole, he applied his brakes and came to an abrupt stop. He didn't need another citation.

He was thinking about his conversation with Kevin earlier that morning, oblivious to what was taking place around him. He was startled by a knock on his window. Mumbling profanity under his breath, he looked up to see the familiar face peering back through the semi-fogged glass. It was him. The haggard homeless guy who had initiated his wild mental detour with his off-beat questions. Joe rolled down his window, somewhat excited to see the stranger again.

"Well?" the stranger inquired bluntly.

"Well, what?" Joe shot back.

"Do you NEED HELP?" he asked, holding up his tattered sign.

"No, I don't need help!" Joe snapped.

"Are you sure?" the man persisted.

"Look, what do you want?"

"Nothing. What do you want?" the vagabond echoed.

"This is crazy! I don't know— maybe you're crazy! Maybe the whole world is crazy! What are you doing here?" Joe rattled his responses off like shots from a Gatling gun.

"Yessir, life can be pretty crazy. Sometimes life just doesn't make much sense. Sometimes what people do doesn't make sense. Sometimes there's just no rhyme or reason— lives lived without purpose. People living in quiet desperation. Know what I mean?"

"No, I don't know what you mean," Joe confessed in frustration.

The cross traffic was coming to a stop. The light was about to change. There was no time to continue the quirky conversation.

"Meet me over there!" Joe directed, motioning to the parking lot on the southwest corner of the intersection. The light turned green. Joe drove through the intersection and turned into the parking lot. He pulled into a parking space, shut off his engine, and got out of his car to wait for the disheveled stranger. When he shut the car door and turned around, the man was standing right in front of him. Joe was startled, but the warmth of the stranger's smile was disarming. Beneath his deeply wrinkled forehead were the kindest eyes he had ever seen. They almost seemed to be twinkling in the afternoon sunlight.

"How did you … oh, never mind," Joe abandoned his train of thought.

"There's a little café just a few doors down. Would you like something to drink?" the homeless man offered.

Joe had a little time before his wife would be expecting him. Though anxious to get home, he was glad to once again see the stranger who had been haunting his thoughts. Maybe now he could get some answers … and, in turn, give his nicely polished response to the original question that had launched this quest.

"Uh—well, I'm not—why don't I—sure, let's go get something to drink." Joe stammered.

7

TABLE TALK

As the two men stood side by side at the counter to order, the vagabond seemed transfixed on the menu board, as if contemplating how he might bet his last dollar at the racetrack.

"What can I get you?" the young man behind the counter asked Joe as he flashed a smile as broad as the Grand Canyon.

"I'm not sure yet. Why don't you take his order first?" Joe replied, pointing to his curious companion.

"Alright, what about you, Sam? What'll it be today?"

Wait. How did he know his name was Sam? Joe wondered. *I'm such a sucker. How many times has this guy conned his way into a free meal? He's obviously been here a lot to be known by name.*

"Let's see. Today I think I'll do a large Café Latte and, if it's alright with you, one of those delightful egg and cheese croissants would be nice," the scruffy character responded.

"Excellent," the cashier said, entering the order into the tablet. "Now back to you. What's your pleasure?" the young man asked as he turned back to Joe.

"You know what—I think I'll have the same."

"A wise choice. Everyone should have what Sam has!" he responded, with a slight grin on his face. "I'll have those orders out to you in just a few minutes. Please make yourselves at home."

"What do I owe you?" Joe asked.

"Oh, this one is on the house since you're a friend of Sam's. Enjoy!"

Joe stood there for a moment, stunned. He wasn't sure what to make of the scene that had just played out before him. He had so many questions swirling in his head, he was semi-paralyzed in thought. He stared at the young man as he simply smiled back at Joe.

"Well, thank you!" Joe finally sputtered.

"My pleasure!" he responded enthusiastically.

"So why don't we get a table and talk," Sam suggested.

Joe followed as Sam shuffled to a quiet table in the back corner of the café, where they both took a seat. Sitting across from one another, Joe noticed a number of things about this familiar stranger. His skin was dark and leathery, as if parched by the desert sun. His hair was long and wiry, but not greasy. His teeth were impressively straight and white. But apart from that, he was indistinct. Joe couldn't figure out his ethnic origin. He could have come from anywhere. His clothes were disheveled and a bit musty but didn't carry the distinct odor that so often accompanied homeless people that he'd encountered. What struck Joe most were his eyes. Sam's eyes were greyish-green and looked as if they could peer into the depths of his soul.

"So, your name is Sam?"

"Sam, I am," he said. "I do not like green eggs and ham."

His comment cut through the obvious tension and brought a smile to both of their faces.

Now a bit more relaxed, Joe dove into what could only be described as an interrogation. "You're obviously no stranger here."

"True. I come here often to meet people and talk."

"Talk about what?"

"Life, love, leadership. It all depends. Sometimes we just talk about finding our way home."

"Finding your way home? But you're homeless."

"Am I?"

"Aren't you?"

"I have a home," Sam stated emphatically.

"Where?"

"Does that really matter?"

"Then why are you on the street corner?"

"To help people."

"Help people? How do you help people?" Joe leaned toward Sam, pressing the question.

"That's yet to be seen."

"What does that mean?" Joe continued to expose his confusion.

"I mean, I help different people in different ways."

"Is that what the sign is about?" Joe asked, pointing to the oversized cardboard calling card now resting against the wall.

"Indeed. I suppose you've picked up on the fact that it's an offer, not a plea."

"It took me awhile, but now I get that!"

"Great. Then how can I help you, Joe?"

"I don't need your help!" Joe stated with an edge of belligerence in his voice.

"Don't you?"

"Why would you think I need your help?" Joe's brow furrowed as the question left his lips.

Sam's eyes narrowed slightly as if peering into a dark closet. After a long pause, he simply said, "Because."

"Because what?" Joe was beginning to lose his patience.

"No, because of Why!" Sam retorted. "Joe, do you remember the question that I asked you when we first met?"

"Of course, I do. It's haunted me ever since. You asked me, 'Why do you do what you do?'"

"Exactly! 'Why?' 'Because' is your answer to 'Why?' Let me ask you again, 'Why do you do what you do?' Your response should be, 'Because....'" Sam's voice trailed off as he let the incomplete sentence hang in the air, making a hand motion in Joe's direction.

"Because it's what I was trained to do. Because it provides for my family. Because it has enabled me to build a great life for myself!" As Joe spoke, his posture changed. He sat up straight in his chair and threw his shoulders back, as if to punctuate his statements with his posture.

"Well said," Sam affirmed. "Indeed, you have provided well for your family, and you've made a good living for yourself. But have you made a good life? There is a significant difference between making a good living and making life good. Is your life making a difference? Is there meaning in your work? Are you living intentionally? You said, you've built 'a good life for yourself,' but does your life have purpose beyond yourself? You see, Joe, your life is a gift to the world!

> *You've made a good living for yourself. But have you made a good life? There is a significant difference between making a good living and making life good.*

And I've discovered that a life wrapped up in itself makes a very small package."

Joe thought it strange that Kevin had said exactly the same thing in their earlier conversation. But before he could think about it further, Sam continued.

"Quality of life isn't found in what you gain from the world, but in what you give to the world. What are you giving back to the world, Joe? Are you truly making a difference outside your closest circle? What kind of legacy will you leave when you depart this planet? How will the world be better *because* you were here?"

Joe sat in stunned silence. He felt he'd just been sucker-punched. He searched the recesses of his mind for what he thought would be an appropriate response but kept coming up empty. Sam let the emptiness fill the air. Finally, Joe spat out a few words.

"My family is my legacy."

"Yes, they are, Joe," Sam said with a glimmer in his eye. "And you have provided well for them over the years. You have given them opportunities well beyond your own. But the greatest gift you can give to them is a sense of responsibility to leave the world a better place than they found it. What kind of a legacy do you want to create for them? How do you want them to view the world? How do you want them to craft meaningful lives? What difference do you want them to make in the world? If you want them to have an impact beyond themselves, you'll have to show them how."

The coffee was beginning to take its effect. Joe excused himself to go to the restroom.

When he returned, Sam was gone.

The cashier who had waited on them earlier informed Joe that something had come up and Sam had to leave unexpectedly. Sam had conveyed his apology and said that he looked forward to continuing the conversation when they saw each other next.

Joe sat down to ponder the conversation he'd just had with Sam. As he sat there, reflecting on what had been said, he found himself staring at the walls of the quaint café.

8

THE TIP

Joe was once again lost in his thoughts when a team member from the café paused at his table to check on his experience.

"I hope you enjoyed your croissant and conversation."

"I did. Thank you so very much. Since your cashier was kind enough to take care of our tab, may I at least leave a tip for the team?" Joe offered.

"That's very kind, but unnecessary. I can pretty much guarantee you that the best tip of the day is the one you just received from Sam."

Joe was beginning to feel as if he was in the crosshairs of a conspiracy. "You obviously know Sam pretty well. Do you have just a minute to talk?"

"Sure," he said as he took a seat at the table.

"So, what's the scoop on Sam?" Joe jumped in.

"Well, I've known Sam for quite a while. The best thing I can tell you is that he leaves a positive wake in the world."

"How long have you known him?"

"Twelve years now. I met him just over there on the street," he said, pointing out the window toward the intersection. "I was going through a very rough patch. I won't bore you with the details but suffice it to say my life was in shambles. I was running from myself with nowhere to go. I wound up living on the streets. I needed help. And, as good fortune would have it, I wound up under that bridge. That's where I met Sam. You could say it was a divine appointment. He took an interest in me and he listened. He saw more in me than I saw in myself. Helped me quit running and turn around to face myself. That's when everything changed."

"What do you mean everything changed?" Joe was being reeled in like a hooked mackerel, tugging on every line that the man uttered.

"Well, to start, he helped me claim my purpose."

There it was again. Every conversation seemed to keep coming back around to purpose.

"Claim your purpose?" Joe asked incredulously. He wanted a more substantive answer.

"Yessir. I finally figured out how to live beyond myself. Up to that point, the only thing I really cared much about was me. I guess you could say the driving question of my life was, *'What's in it for me?'* If it didn't affect me, I didn't really care. And if it did affect me, that was all I really cared about. But then I ran into Sam. He asked me what I wanted to do with my life. It was a strange question, given that I was living on the streets. Soon, Sam had me convinced that I could make a real difference in the world, if only I could look beyond myself. That's when we opened the café."

Every day I do what I can to make someone's day just a little bit better. I want to contribute to making their story better, even if just for a moment.

"So, you're the owner?"

"I guess you could say it's a joint venture. I *own* everyone's experience when they come through those doors. My purpose is to create an environment where people can connect with themselves and others in meaningful ways. Every day I do what I can to make someone's day just a little bit better. I want to contribute to making their story better, even if just for a moment. No one comes through those doors by accident. I believe that every encounter is a divine appointment, and every moment is a chance to make the world just a little bit better. So, yes, I have responsibility for making this little café the best café for those who are kind enough to spend some of their time here. But Sam actually owns the café."

Joe's mouth fell open and his eyes widened. "Sam owns the café? Then why is he hanging out at the intersection with a cardboard sign?"

"You mean the sign that says, 'Need Help?' Oh, that's his signature question. That and 'Why do you do what you do?' Both are great questions. Once you get over your pride and answer the first question honestly—we all need a little help—then maybe you'll have enough humility to consider the second one. Sam wanted to create a place where people could contemplate both questions. And, well, he picked that intersection."

For the first time Joe allowed his eyes to explore his present environment. The bright sign above the entrance identified the establishment as the Coincidence Café. Questions and sayings, written in a familiar style, adorned the walls: "Everyone can make a difference in the world. How will you?" "Everyone has a purpose. What's yours?" "Why do you do what you do?" But the one that really caught Joe's attention read, "Coincidence is just God's way of remaining anonymous."

"What is that supposed to mean?" Joe asked, pointing to what he had just read on the wall.

"Well, I've come to believe that life is filled with meaning and purpose. Some say God created it that way by design. If you believe that, then it's not hard to believe that God is constantly trying to speak to each one of us. He's trying to get our attention off ourselves to see that there is much to be done in the world around us. People often think that things happen by chance. But the truth may be that God is nudging us to notice things we've failed to see before. We call them a coincidence because we have no other way of explaining them. Experiences seem randomly connected. Maybe there's more meaning and purpose behind events than we think. Maybe there's more to life than just

> *People often think that things happen by chance. But the truth may be that God is nudging us to notice things we've failed to see before*

getting through the day and getting as much as we can for ourselves." With that he paused, letting Joe sit for a moment and soak in what he had said.

Joe scoured the room as if looking for the missing piece to complete a puzzle. Each question seemed to jump off the wall as he retraced them in his mind. He wondered what kind of a difference he could make. He questioned what his purpose could possibly be. Did he really have one beyond himself? Was it a coincidence that he had bumped into Sam or was there more at play? The questions swirled in his head like a dust devil on the Oklahoma plains.

His thoughts were rudely interrupted by the vibration of his phone on the café table. The call was from his wife, Kathy. He excused himself and stepped outside to take the call so as not to disturb the other patrons. She was letting him know that the hospital had called about his father. The nurse had urged them to come quickly. Kathy said she was dropping everything to meet him there. It was the call Joe dreaded, though it was not altogether unexpected.

Joe had always had a somewhat strained relationship with his father. While he respected his success as a business leader, he resented the fact that his father had been physically and emotionally absent as Joe was growing up. Joe felt that his father, even though highly regarded in the corporate community, had in many ways abandoned his family. His workaholism and alcoholism had strained every relationship he had. Ultimately, it was his unfaithfulness that led to Joe's mother divorcing him. After the divorce, the only contact he had with his father was when he would occasionally pay for Joe and his brother to join him on trips to desirable destinations. But it never made up for all of the ball games and school activities he had missed due to his heavy travel schedule. Eventually, Joe's brother chose to distance himself from the continual disappointment. Joe alone was left to care for his father, which was a duty he assumed reluctantly. Now, apparently, that responsibility might be short-lived.

Without hesitation, he bolted to his car, never thinking to thank his host or explain his hasty departure.

9

THE LEGACY

Joe made his way through the maze of hallways at the hospital until he found Kathy in the waiting room of the CCU. Her face revealed her concern. As she explained what the doctor had told her, a nurse entered the room.

"Are you Joe?" she asked.

"Yes," he replied.

"Your father is asking to see you. Will you please follow me?"

Joe kissed Kathy and followed the nurse into a private room. His father was hooked up to monitors tracking his vital signs. The beeping of the machines was an ever-present reminder of his critical condition. The nurse raised the head of his bed slightly and removed his oxygen mask so he could speak.

"Hey Son. I'm glad you're here. It means a lot to me," he said, laboring with each short breath. "I wanted to see you."

"Of course, Dad. I'm here for you."

"I know. And it's ironic. I wasn't always there for you. I'm sorry, Joe," tears coming to his eyes as he spoke. "When you're facing death, you see life differently. I've been thinking." Each sentence took some effort. "I've come to some sobering realizations. At the end, money and things don't matter. It's about people. It's how you treat them. That's what really matters. Do you know what I mean, Joe?"

> *When you're facing death, you see life differently. At the end, money and things don't matter. It's about people. It's how you treat them. That's what really matters.*

"I think I do, Dad," Joe responded in a comforting tone.

"I just wanted you to know how very much I love you. I'm so proud of you. And please tell your brother I love him too!"

"I will, Dad."

"And, Joe," his father paused for a moment to formulate what he wanted to say. "Please promise me you'll live a better life than I did. Give to others, son. Make a difference in someone's world. Don't just make a good living, make life good. I wasn't a great example for you, but I can pass on the challenge."

Joe was beginning to freak out a bit. The words sounded eerily similar to the conversation he had with Sam a short while earlier. Maintaining his composure, Joe simply nodded and said, "I love you, Dad."

With that, the nurse interrupted the conversation. "He needs his rest now," she said, as she put the oxygen mask back over his nose and mouth.

Joe's father reached for his hand. Joe clasped it firmly, as if to reinforce the commitments he'd just made.

Joe's father squeezed his hand and then let go. Joe returned to Kathy in the waiting room and was shocked to see Sam standing there talking with Kathy.

"Wow, what are you doing here, Sam?!" Joe was beside himself.

"Oh, I come here occasionally. Sorry I left you alone at the café. I lost track of time and needed to be here. I made a promise to your dad that I would come see him as soon as the evening visiting hours began."

"But how did you know he was my dad?" Joe was seriously perplexed.

"I didn't know he was your dad until recently. Kathy and I were just putting some of the pieces together. Quite a coincidence, wouldn't you say, Joe? I left his room not long before you arrived. How was your conversation with him? He was very concerned about you getting here. He said there were some things he really needed to tell you."

"To be honest, the conversation sounded a lot like ours at the cafe, Sam," Joe responded. "Not at all what I expected to hear from my father."

Sam's eyes were piercing and his tone somber as he replied, "Well, maybe the legacy has now begun!"

Joe's mind was about to explode. But just as he prepared to launch into another long list of questions for Sam, the doctor entered the waiting room. The doctor graciously interrupted and began to discuss with Kathy and Joe his father's condition. The prognosis wasn't good. After answering several questions, the doctor excused himself to finish his rounds. When Joe finally turned to address Sam, he was gone once again.

10

In Search of the Wizard

The next day Joe found himself staring at the same question on the corkboard in the break room at work as Kevin entered for his morning coffee.

"Good morning, Joe. I'm sorry to hear about your dad. You and the family are certainly in my thoughts and prayers. Please let me know if I can do anything to help," Kevin offered.

Wow, word certainly gets around fast, Joe thought to himself before responding. "Actually, there is something you can do, Kevin. Can you come into my office for a few minutes?"

"Of course!" Kevin replied without hesitation.

Once they entered his office, Joe closed the door behind him. He motioned toward the table in the corner of the room and they both took a seat.

"I don't really know where to begin," Joe started. "This whole week has been really weird. Some things have happened that have me thinking about what I'm doing with my life. It's strange. I thought I was living the dream. But now, I'm not so sure. It's like my whole world has been caught up in a tornado and I'm not sure where or how I'm going to land."

"You mean like Dorothy and Toto?" Kevin asked.

"Alright, that's the second time this week you've mentioned Dorothy. Have you been to see *Wicked* recently, or are you just obsessed with *The Wizard of Oz*?"

"No, but I have been reading the story to my kids. And I've been thinking too! Each one of the characters needed something different. Do you remember what the Scarecrow needed?"

"Of course—he needed a brain," Joe responded.

"And the Tin Man?"

"Well, he needed a heart."

"Right. And the Lion?" Kevin continued.

"He needed courage."

"Correct, again. But in the end, they each discovered that they already had everything they needed to complete their journey. The Scarecrow possessed practical wisdom and common sense, making him the most adept at problem solving. The Tin Man demonstrated great heart. And the Lion wound up being the bravest of them all. Maybe the moral to the story is that when we join forces to find our way in the world, we discover our purpose. That purpose awakens the parts of us that have been dormant. Like Dorothy and her trio, we discover that there's no wizard pulling the strings behind the scenes. Rather, each of us must assume personal responsibility to dismantle evil in the world and create for ourselves an *Emerald City*.

Life is not meant to be a solo sport. We are all connected in this global community. There is only one race that matters, and that's the human race.

You see, Joe, life is not meant to be a solo sport. We are all connected in this global community. There is only one race that matters, and that's the human race. And every member of the human race should be a change agent for good. You know, we often speak of changing the world. But honestly, that seems like a rather daunting task. But like I said earlier, instead of trying to change the whole world, maybe we should focus instead on changing the world for one person. If each and every one of us changed the world for one other person, we would indeed be changing the world! Maybe we don't need a wizard to give us what we need. Maybe we need to give of ourselves to someone else. And, in giving to someone else, we may very well find what we need ourselves. Lately I've been asking myself, 'Who is my someone?'"

"Since when did you become such a philosopher?" Joe asked.

"Sorry, I got a little carried away. It's just that all of this stuff has been rattling around in my head for a while now. That's why I posted the question in the break room. I'm trying to answer questions like, 'What am I doing?' 'Why am I here?' And 'What's my purpose?'"

"So that's the origin of the mysterious sign!" Joe smirked.

"Well, sort of. It all actually started some time ago. It's a quirky story. Late one afternoon, I was lost in my own thoughts while driving home from work. As often happens, I was stopped at an intersection when I noticed a drifter holding a cardboard sign that read, 'Need Help?'"

"Oh, come on!" Joe reacted. "You've got to be kidding me! Seriously, am I on *Candid Camera?* This is a joke, right? Did Sam put you up to this?"

"You know Sam?" Kevin asked with excitement.

"He's the one that screwed up my world. I thought I was happy until I met him. Now, I'm questioning my very existence. Sam *is* the tornado that turned my world upside down!" Joe exclaimed in exasperation. This has got to be the craziest...," Joe hesitated.

"Coincidence," Kevin said, completing his sentence.

The two sat there staring at one another as if they had just debunked the Da Vinci Code. Finally, Kevin broke the silence. "So, I guess you're just like the rest of us – you 'Need Help' too," he said, making air quotes with his fingers.

"I didn't think I did, but maybe I do," Joe admitted. "What about you? What help do you need? You seem to have it all together!"

"'Seem' is the operative word there, Joe. Oh, don't get me wrong, my life is good. I love my wife and kids. My job is fulfilling. I'm happy. But there was something nagging me internally. I kept wondering if maybe there was more to life. Does that make any sense?" Kevin asked.

"It makes a lot of sense. And something else haunts me," Joe chimed in. "If I'm honest, sometimes I feel like an imposter. I've got everything I could possibly want and yet I'm still not satisfied. I put on this front like life is just grand, but at times it seems shallow and empty. I don't really feel that I'm making a difference in the world. Funny thing is that for a long time I did a pretty darn good job of suppressing these feelings. That is, until the tornado hit! Sam has really messed with my head!" Joe stated emphatically.

"Or maybe he's just touched your heart!" Kevin chimed in. Both men sat there for a moment as if frozen in time. Joe broke the silence.

"So, let's get back to Sam," Joe redirected the conversation. "What happened after you met him?"

"For weeks – nothing! I didn't see him again. But the question, '*Why do you do what you do?*' sent me into a tailspin. I came up with several answers to that question, but none of them seemed satisfactory. 'To take care of my family.' 'To make a ton of money.' 'To retire to the lake.' Those were all the answers that came to mind. But then I had to ask myself, 'So what?' I mean, in the long run, what difference would it make if I died in a lake house? What legacy would I have created if I merely left my kids a bunch of money? Who would care? What good would I have done in the world?

"There had to be more to life than simply breathing the Earth's air and consuming its resources, fritting away my time trying to make a good living. I wanted to make life good. I know that sounds crazy, but his question was driving me crazy! Then one day, I saw him again at the intersection. He invited me to have coffee."

"At the Coincidence Café," Joe finished Kevin's statement.

"You've been there?"

"Yep, with Sam. But only long enough to finish a croissant and get jilted!" Joe laughed.

"Sam does have a tendency to come and go as he pleases," Kevin acknowledged. "And since that first conversation, I've become a regular patron of the café. I rarely see Sam, but I meet the most interesting people there. And we usually have some pretty deep conversations. It's almost as if it's a think tank for great service ideas."

"Service ideas?"

"Well sometimes I'll meet someone, and we just talk about life's issues. But, on a number of occasions, the conversation has turned toward how we could truly make a difference in our respective communities. We find a problem and try to solve it.

I've heard some pretty fascinating ideas. Actually, some that *I've* thought were pretty crazy. But what's crazier still is that many of them start to become reality. Someone will introduce someone to someone else who has a similar passion and before you know it, the parts start coming together. Some of the ideas were, well, pretty crazy—until they weren't. It's really astonishing if you sit back and look at it," Kevin declared.

"So, people are coming together to follow the yellow brick road!" Joe interjected.

"Nice. I see what you did there," Kevin affirmed. "Hey, would you be interested in joining me at the Coincidence Café for lunch on Friday. A small group of folks get together at noon just to hang out and talk. You're more than welcome to come, if you'd like."

"How can I say no? I'm already knee-deep. I may as well jump into the surf. Let's ride over together. Just stop by here on Friday when you're ready to go."

11

On the Way to the Café

The rest of the week was a blur for Joe. Friday came quickly. As promised, Kevin showed up at his office door a little before noon.

"Ready to go?" Kevin invited.

"Let's do this!" was Joe's eager reply.

The two men walked to the parking lot and jumped in Joe's car. On the trip to the café, Joe peppered Kevin with more questions.

"So, who do you expect to show up today. Any influencers that I might know?" Joe was always interested in opportunities to connect with other business leaders.

"It's always a different group. Most of the time it's just common folks like you and me. Occasionally someone will be there that I recognize as a corporate bigshot or an elected official. It varies, but it's always interesting to see the mix of people who show up."

"How often do you go?"

"I typically make it once or twice a month. There's no formal commitment. Just show up as you can. The café provides lunch. You can leave ten bucks in the basket to cover the cost, if you like. Most folks do, but not everyone. For some, it's 'on the house.'" Kevin noted.

Joe thought that was interesting.

"What do they typically talk about?" Joe probed.

"It's always different. I rarely know in advance. But I always leave with a lot to think about. And often with a new friend or two."

"So, it's a great place to network?"

"In a way, but it's a little different."

"How so?"

"They actually refer to it as *Net-Weaving*. The idea is that everyone comes with a spirit of seeking to connect people with similar passion to do good. In other words, instead of trying to tell your story or press your agenda, you seek to listen intently to someone else's story in the hopes of being able to connect that person with someone in your circle of influence who may help to advance a worthy cause. Everyone comes together with a spirit of giving rather than receiving. Most people are only a few introductions away from fulfilling a dream. And you may actually play a part in helping make the introductions that cause a dream to become a reality.

Most people are only a few introductions away from fulfilling a dream. And you may actually play a part in helping make the introductions that cause a dream to become a reality.

"It's sort of like playing with Legos. Every person comes to the table with their own blocks. The fun is in trying to snap our blocks together in a way that creates greater value." Kevin explained. "It's fascinating and fun to see what can be built and what good can come from simply pooling our resources for a specific purpose."

As they pulled up to *the* intersection, they both scanned the area for any sight of Sam. Not today. No Sam and no sign. When the light turned green, Joe drove through the intersection and made a familiar turn into the parking lot. There were quite a few more cars than the last time he had parked here. As they got out of his car, Joe locked the doors behind him, twice. Each time, the car's security system chirped. Kevin looked at Joe quizzically.

"What? I'm just making sure that it's locked. There are a lot of homeless people around here, you know!"

"Right," said Kevin with a skeptical glance. "Oh, and nice license plate, by the way!"

12

Coincidence Café

The tables were filled with people enjoying a good meal and each other's company. Kevin led Joe to a small private room toward the back of the café. In the room were a dozen or so people standing around engaged in animated conversation.

A young lady welcomed them and encouraged them to write their names on a nametag. No sooner had they placed the nametags on their shirts than they were greeted by a man who invited them into a circle of conversation. After a few minutes of introductions and superficial chat, a young man formally welcomed everyone and introduced himself as Hunter, a co-owner of the café.

Joe recognized him immediately. It was the same young man who had spoken to him after Sam's vanishing act.

So his name is Hunter, Joe thought to himself. He had never asked his name.

Hunter introduced the lady who had initially greeted them at the door. Her name was Susan, and she too was a co-owner of the café. He lauded her for her ability to create environments that were warm and welcoming. And he gave her credit for the wonderful lunch that was about to be served. With that, he invited everyone to help themselves to the buffet tables at the back of the room.

The conversations continued as each person moved through the line and made their strategic selections. The presentation was impressive for such a small group. Decorated nicely with freshly cut flowers, the tables held a sumptuous smorgasbord of entrees. Not your typical array of deli meats to make a quick sandwich, this was truly a culinary cornucopia.

At the end of the buffet tables sat a basket into which most people placed some money. On the basket, a sign read, "Suggested donation: $10." Joe reached into his pocket and extracted a ten spot. When he dropped it into the basket, he noticed most of the donations were 20-dollar bills and there were three 100-dollar bills that were visible. *Quite a generous group*, he thought as he made a mental note.

Several tables set for four people dotted the room. On each table was a card with a couple of questions that guided the table discussion as they ate. The questions were curious and prompted some very interesting conversation among the four newfound friends. When enough time had passed to allow everyone to eat, Hunter stood once again and announced the topic for what he called the "Coincidental Conversation" for the day.

"Our topic today is 'Ending Homelessness,'" he announced. "Who would like to begin by asking questions of clarification?"

Joe glanced over at Kevin with a look of surprise. He leaned over and whispered, "This group is going to solve the problem of homelessness in an hour?"

Kevin just grinned.

The first question came from a stately-looking gentleman in his mid-fifties, wearing a fashionable gray suit with complementary tie and pocket handkerchief. "Are we talking about globally or locally."

From another table a woman quickly chimed in, "I think it's always beneficial to talk globally and seek to act locally."

Several people nodded their heads in agreement.

"How many of you've been stopped on the street corner by a homeless person asking for money?" The query was posed by a man who appeared to be in his early forties. His clothing was clean but modest. His hair was long and pulled back in a ponytail. Joe noticed earlier that he hadn't placed any money in the basket.

Every hand in the room went up in response to his question.

"And how many of you've given people like that some money?"

Again, almost every hand was raised.

"Why would you do that?" he asked sincerely.

There was a protracted pause. And then, like popcorn, people started to respond.

"To help someone a little."

"Because I can," said another.

"To share what I have to meet a need."

"To ease someone's suffering."

"I'm sorry, but that all sounds like a bunch of crap," the man blurted out. "I challenge you to look deeper within and be more honest."

Again, silence filled the room. Joe could feel his heart racing and his neck getting warm. He felt strangely uncomfortable.

He was glad that he hadn't said anything yet. He tried to reflect upon his motivation when he had given Sam the $10 that was sitting in his cup holder. In thinking back on it, he was embarrassed about telling him not to spend it on alcohol. He had judged him without asking a single question. He certainly had no interest in hearing his story.

The same lady who had made the comment about "acting locally" was the first to confess: "I suppose I give so that I don't have to truly engage with that person. It assuages my conscience so that I can simply move on with my life without being delayed."

"OK. I appreciate your honesty," he affirmed.

"Well, if I'm going to be candid," another said, "I don't give at all because I think that person is probably going to waste it on drugs or alcohol. I don't want to enable that kind of behavior. And I've seen countless charlatans. You know, people who are just preying on people's sympathy. There are lots of crazy and lazy people out there who would rather beg than actually work."

"Yep," the ponytailed stranger conceded. "You'd be right. A lot of folks make more money begging than they could from countless jobs. Think about it. If only two or three people slowed down long enough to toss them a ten, that's far more than they could make flippin' burgers or washing windows! And some of those folks are so convincing they can get more in one day of begging than they could working a whole week!"

"So, what are you saying?" the man in the suit asked. "We shouldn't try to help?"

"I'm not saying that at all," the modest man countered. "But is that really helping? Throwing money and resources haphazardly at a problem is a pretty foolish approach to finding a solution, wouldn't you say? In reality, it's pretty heartless. Do you throw money so you don't have to get involved? Or is it just your way of tipping fate, thankful that you're fortunate enough not to be on the other side?"

The last question nailed Joe between the eyes. That was it. That was exactly why he'd given Sam ten bucks. It was his attempt to manipulate fate. Through his benevolence he saw himself as somehow bartering for better karma. But his pittance only puffed up his pride. He had judged Sam as being inferior before he ever took the time to get to know him. Joe slumped somewhat in his chair.

13

A Chance

"Besides, a conscience-clearing contribution on the street corner isn't going to solve anything!" the humble philosopher continued. "What's really needed is a *hand up*, not a *handout*. People who want a handout are living off a broken system that is unsustainable. They don't become independent. They simply become more dependent upon a system that enslaves them. That cycle must be broken. If it's not, eventually an insane number of resources will be required to fuel faulty programs."

"Then what do you suggest?" the man in the suit asked sincerely.

"Get involved," the lady at Joe's table contributed. "There are a ton of opportunities in the community—shelters, food kitchens, clothing distribution centers. But the best groups are those that have a rehabilitation strategy at the heart of their services. They help people get sober. They train people with skills and provide job-matching opportunities. That way they aren't just providing food and shelter, but they're providing a chance at a better life. They emphasize accountability, dignity, self-worth, and independence as their objectives."

"I've been to many of those shelters," another chimed in. "What I can tell you is that many of the folks who seek out those services have no interest in working to make a better life for themselves. They have become so dependent upon handouts that they have no motivation. Many are quite content with their situation. They wouldn't work, even if they had the opportunity."

"Precisely," said the man who had instigated this whole disruptive conversation. Apparently, he was now the discussion leader. "I can tell you from my personal experience that's a fact. That's exactly where I was. I was lost. I couldn't see my way through the week. I sank into a severe depression after losing my wife to cancer. I was completely debilitated. I self-medicated. Soon, I lost my job and shortly after that, I lost my home. I really had no place to turn. I had no family to speak of and I was too embarrassed to turn to friends, so I just hit the road. And then, I hit bottom. After driving across the country, my car broke down and my funds ran out. I found myself on the streets. I had no motivation to do anything. I just didn't care about life anymore. I subsisted. I panhandled. My spirit was broken because I had lost my dignity. I wouldn't have taken a job if you'd offered it to me. I had no meaning, no direction or purpose in life. I just wanted to end the pain. So I tried to take my own life."

The room fell silent. For the first time, Joe noticed the scars on his wrists, which were only partially covered by the sleeves of his ill-fitting shirt. Joe wondered how such a bright and articulate person could ever succumb to such a mental and emotional collapse. But he was even more taken aback by his vulnerability. It was extremely courageous of him to share his struggles so openly.

"I was lying in the hospital when this guy entered my room. At first, I thought I was hallucinating. We talked briefly and he said he would come back again soon. I really thought it had all been a dream. But the next day, when I was more lucid, he showed up again. We talked for hours. I felt comfortable because he seemed to be like me. He listened to my story with understanding. He empathized. And then he asked me, 'What do you want out of life?' My response was, 'Nothing. I simply want *out of life!*' The man smiled back at me with a look of understanding. There was no judgment, only compassion in his eyes.

"He didn't try to talk me out of my misery or try and convince me that life wasn't that bad. Instead, he gave me hope by redirecting my thoughts. He said, 'I suspect what you're looking for is happiness. But happiness pursued eludes. Happiness that's given returns. And the only way to stop the pain is by moving into the suffering of someone else and seeking to understand. Life is about more than you. It's about what you're doing for others. Your life has lost meaning because you're focused entirely on yourself. Your depression is the result of grieving without hope. When you lost your wife, you had no other avenue through which to channel your love, so your heart dried up. It's a heart issue. It has nothing to do with what's happening around you, but rather what's happening in you. There has to be a shift on the inside for life to become rich.' Then he summed it all up by saying, 'Life isn't about getting rich. It's

> *Happiness pursued eludes. Happiness that's given returns.*

about being rich. Rich relationally, rich emotionally, rich spiritually. Richness in life comes from doing good for others.'"

"Wow, that's really powerful," Joe blurted out before he could catch himself. "Did you ever find out who that man was?"

"Of course," he replied. "He's one of the co-owners of this café and he's seated right beside you."

Joe turned to the man seated to his right. He had earlier introduced himself as Dusty. He said he owned an auto repair shop

> *Life isn't about getting rich. It's about being rich. Rich relationally, rich emotionally, rich spiritually. Richness in life comes from doing good for others.*

nearby called Classic Car Care and invited Joe to stop by sometime.

"He also owns a car repair shop," he continued. "I just started working there a couple of weeks ago. I'm grateful for the opportunity and I'm learning a lot. Not just about fixing cars, but about helping to fix other people's problems by creating as much value for them as I possibly can. It's all kinda new to me, but I finally have a reason to get up in the morning."

"That's great, Dusty," Joe acknowledged, addressing his new friend.

"Yes, it is, Joe," Dusty replied. "Great for me! We both had a need and we filled it for one another. I needed someone else to help in the shop and Justin needed a chance. All I did was find a good person to whom I could offer a chance. Don't get me wrong. It's not something I could or would do for everyone."

The gentleman in the suit re-engaged in the conversation with a follow up question for Dusty: "So, if I may ask, how do you decide who is worthy of a chance?"

"That can be a bit tricky," Dusty admitted. "You can only help those who want to be helped and who are willing to take personal responsibility for making things better. There are lots of folks who want a better life, but not everyone's willing to work hard at getting better at life. Some play the role of the victim. Others are simply looking for a handout. Some are con men who are trying to play you. The only way to know for sure is to take the time to find out what's in the heart of that person. You have to be curious. You have to get involved and listen to their story. It can't be a quick transaction. It has to start with a genuine relationship. But the biggest factor for me is whether or not that person is willing to learn. Are they hungry? Are they open to feedback? Are they quick to apply what they are learning? If so, then skills can be taught."

The conversation lasted for another half-hour or so. Joe's mind was reeling, and his heart was heavy. He was feeling a strange blend of conviction and excitement. For far too long he had skimmed through life, never really slowing down long enough to see or acknowledge the countless needs around him. He had walked through life with blinders on. Down deep, maybe he just didn't want to see the problems. After all, he had enough of his own, so it was easier to ignore the challenges of others. But he also felt excited. He wondered how Dusty must feel knowing he had made such a critical difference in someone else's life. He began to wonder how he might possibly do the same.

14

DATE NIGHT

The weekend finally arrived. Joe had been looking forward to his evening with Kathy. Years ago, the couple designated Friday as "Date Night," their weekly attempt to stay emotionally connected and discuss important matters. Tonight, Kathy had made reservations at one of their favorite spots.

When they arrived, the hostess escorted them to a quiet table on the patio near the firepit. After ordering drinks and appetizers, Joe initiated the conversation.

"I've been doing a lot of thinking lately about our lives. I wonder if there might be more we could do to help others in our community."

"I'm listening," Kathy responded, as she leaned forward.

"I don't know. I mean we've got a good life, right? But my time with Dad the other day at the hospital really rocked my world. Kathy, I've never heard him talk like that before. He was challenging me to do better with my life than he has with his own. He was talking about leaving a legacy and doing good for others. I'm pretty sure Sam is in the mix somehow. I know I'm rambling, but are we setting a good example for the kids? Or am I becoming my father? I know I'm a good provider financially, but am I living in a way that inspires our children to really make a difference in the world? *Am I* making a difference in the world? Honest to God, I think I'm having a mid-life meltdown."

Kathy sat patiently listening to Joe's meandering musings until she thought it appropriate to interject. "First, you are a wonderful provider! Thank you for taking such good care of us. We have a good life. And no, you are not your father. But I am actually excited to hear you talking about what good we might possibly do for others. Remember when we served at the women's shelter? The kids still talk about that. And I would love to think of other ways we could do more for those in need. Actually, my mind has often thought about what it would be like to adopt a child."

"Whoa, whoa, whoa! Slow down, Sweetheart. You're *way* ahead of me. You do realize that we aren't spring chickens anymore, don't you? There's no way we could handle a baby at our age. I'd be in a wheelchair at his high school graduation!"

"I know, but there are so many older kids in foster care who need a loving and stable environment. We have extra room at the house. And I think the kids would be all in on the idea," Kathy offered, her eyes twinkling.

"I was thinking more like serving in the kitchen at the shelter a couple of times a year. You're talking about a life-altering commitment!"

"Well, isn't that what we're talking about here – altering someone's life. How are we going to alter someone else's life if it doesn't alter ours?"

Joe never expected such a response from Kathy. Now he was wondering if he had inadvertently opened Pandora's box. He was bewildered. Kathy sensed his discomfort and dialed it back a notch.

"I could tell that something has been on your mind. I'm sorry that you're struggling. But I have to tell you I'm excited about where this may lead. We can explore the possibilities slowly, as we both feel comfortable. We don't have to rush into anything. Right now, let's just enjoy dinner," Kathy said as she smiled graciously.

Joe felt a huge weight lifted. He was grateful for Kathy's understanding and empathy toward his struggle. He was grappling with some deep issues, but he wasn't quite ready to give away the farm. Doing a little good was one thing; changing his lifestyle was something altogether different.

They shifted the conversation to other family matters. The warmth from the fire offset the chill in the night air. The meal and the service were both impeccable. It was the perfect way to wind down the week.

After dessert, Joe paid the bill, tipping more generously than usual. As they stood to leave, Joe held Kathy's chair. He was helping her into her jacket when she smiled and said, "And by the way, I really like Sam. He's an interesting guy—very insightful."

15

DO FOR ONE

The next morning, Joe made a quick trip to the office. It was unusual for him to go in on a Saturday, but he had to get some files for a meeting across town on Monday. As he left the office, he remembered Dusty's offer to pop in whenever he was in the area. Since Classic Car Care wasn't too far out of his way, he decided to drop by to see if Dusty might be there.

He pulled into the parking lot a little before noon. Classic Car Care was a modest building, but clean and well-kept. As he entered the front door, he was impressed with the décor: nice leather seating, a glass-top coffee table on a decorative wrought iron pedestal, and beautifully framed pictures of vintage cars adorning the walls. It was not at all what he expected to see in the waiting area of a car repair shop. He asked the lady behind the counter if Dusty was around. She said that he was in the shop but that she would be happy to go get him. While she did, Joe thumbed through the current copy of the *Harvard Business Review* lying on the coffee table. He thought it a bit odd for the *HBR* to be preferred reading material in such an establishment. Nevertheless, he found an article of interest, took a seat, and began to read.

"Joe, I'm so glad you took me up on my offer!" Dusty's voice interrupted his reading. "Hey, come here a minute. There's somebody in the shop who'd like to see you," he said, motioning for Joe to follow him.

As they entered the shop, Joe was even more impressed. A few classic cars dotted the bays. The empty service areas were immaculate. Not a single oil spot marred the garage floor, which gleamed with the logos of automobile manufacturers from bygone eras. So engrossed in surveying the shop, Joe accidentally bumped into Dusty when he stopped walking.

"You remember Justin from our lunch meeting yesterday," Dusty prompted.

"Of course I do. But we didn't get a chance to personally meet," Joe responded.

The truth was that he had met just about everyone else at the lunch meeting. But after noticing Justin didn't put any money in the basket, Joe sized him up unfairly. Joe made the decision not to make the effort to introduce himself the day before. Now, he was feeling rather foolish.

"I really appreciate you sharing your story yesterday. It was quite inspirational. I hope things work out well for you here," Joe said, referring to the shop.

"Oh, I'm sure they will. I just keep looking for problems to solve. You know, the bigger the problem you solve, the more value you create. The more value you create, the more invaluable you become," Justin offered, smiling at Dusty. "Something I learned from a good coach!"

> *The bigger the problem you solve, the more value you create. The more value you create, the more invaluable you become.*

Dusty and Justin exchanged fist bumps.

"Come on, Joe," Dusty said, "let's go chat in my office."

With that, Dusty and Joe made their way back across the shop floor, through the waiting area, and into a modest but nicely appointed office. Pictures of family and friends adorning the shelves and walls revealed that Dusty was relationally rich. Rather than sitting behind his desk, Dusty gestured toward a table in the corner and offered Joe a chair. While Joe took his seat, Dusty reached into the closet and retrieved two bottles of water from a small refrigerator. Joe couldn't contain his curiosity any longer. As Dusty handed him a cold bottle, he started blurting out questions.

"I'm curious. What did you see in Justin that made you want to hire him?"

"That's a great question," Dusty responded. "But I have to back up a bit. It really all started when I was challenged to take the time to find out what he was all about. I was introduced to Justin through a mutual friend named Sam, one of the owners of the Coincidence Café."

"I know Sam," Joe offered. He wondered momentarily just how wide Sam's web had been spun and how many lives he could possibly have impacted.

"Well, Sam challenged me to see whether or not Justin might be a horse worth betting on. So we met at the café for me to hear his story."

"And what about his story impressed you?" Joe asked.

"You saw yesterday how vulnerable he is. Justin is an open book. Vulnerability is courageous. There's no posturing or pretense. He was hurting and he didn't mind others knowing.

At the same time, he was open to feedback. If I made a suggestion, he responded to it. If I offered an insight, he inquired further. If I challenged him, he stepped up to meet it. He was hungry. He simply lacked the will and an opportunity. Life had beaten him down. He had lost connection with any constructive community. But I sensed he was teachable. So I hired him."

"Just like that?"

"Yessir, just like that!"

"But did he have any experience or expertise in working on cars?"

"Nope. But that wasn't necessary. I've learned that competencies are often overrated.

Someone may be highly competent, have a great resume and vast experience, but if they're lazy, they lack an openness to feedback, or they're a *prima donna*, then they can be toxic. No matter how much experience and expertise they may have, their presence can be detrimental. On the other hand, if they're hungry and teachable, they can learn most anything."

"But you said that Justin lacked will. Isn't that the same as being lazy?" Joe pressed.

"Again, that's a very insightful question that's worth exploring," Dusty affirmed. "Justin wasn't lazy. He lacked the will because he had lost sight of his purpose. When he lost his wife, he lost his sense of direction. She *was* his world. We're all designed to connect deeply with others and, for him, she was his only connection to purpose. He loved her deeply. When he lost

> *Love gives. Love is sacrificial.*

her, he thought he had lost his only chance to give of himself to someone else. Love gives. Love is sacrificial. At the time I met him, Justin lacked meaningful avenues through which to express his love. When you don't express love, the heart dries up. You become isolated and lonely because you've insulated yourself from meaningful connections with others. And that's exactly what had happened to Justin. He didn't know where else to express his gifts, talents, and passion. He lost his connection with humanity. And, in doing so, he lost his connection with himself. He lost his purpose. Once he found his purpose again, his enthusiasm and motivation skyrocketed."

> *Our purpose in life is to create value for others. To make a difference in the world. To make the human condition better. To make the world a better place.*

"What did he discover was his purpose?"

"The same as for each one of us!" Dusty exclaimed. "Our purpose in life is to create value for others. To make a difference in the world. To make the human condition better. To make the world a better place. It doesn't matter what you do or whom you do it for, it's simply a matter of doing good for others. A life lived for self makes little difference in the world.

> *There is an old proverb that says, 'The one who is lazy is akin to those who are self-destructive.*

A life lived for self leaves no lasting legacy. Purpose is found in discovering what you have to give to make the planet a better place. And that's not dependent upon race, creed, color, gender, or vocation. It's about character and connectivity. It's all about your willingness to grow and to give."

"Alright, I'll bite," Joe interjected. "But you can't do that for everyone. So how do you decide who gets the good fortune to be the recipient of your benevolent efforts?"

"First, you eliminate laziness. There is an old proverb that says, 'The one who is lazy is akin to those who are self-destructive.' There are people everywhere who seek handouts, or they've become dependent upon the system. If they're satisfied with that, move on! If they're unwilling to work to make their situation better, you can't help them. You'll be wasting your time, energy, and resources if you try. Others see themselves as victims, or they feel entitled. Again, move on! If they blame others, it means they refuse to take personal responsibility for making positive change. Such deflection of responsibility only leads to dependence. You can never grow a sustainable solution if lazy people are allowed to prey upon the system. If someone isn't willing to make a contribution to be a part of the solution, it isn't sustainable. In other words, a system of value creation will never work if you have an overload of value extractors. If everyone takes more off the table than they bring, then it won't be too long until there's nothing left on the table," Dusty explained. His insights were clear, concise, and compelling.

"So basically, no system is sustainable if you have more people taking than you have giving in the equation. Is that what you're saying?"

"Of course. It's rather self-evident, isn't it? We have broken systems all around us.

Governmental systems suffer from political partisanship that creates dependency to secure their voter base. Corporate programs, while well-intentioned, are often not seen as part of the solution. Philanthropic institutions, which are also well-meaning, often lack the capacity to drive sustainable change. Foundations that dispense dollars with little accountability are inadequate. Other entities miss the opportunity to back potentially positive disruptive methodologies because they demand proof of effectiveness before they dispense dollars, leaving creative concepts to languish without support. Many wealthy people operate on the mistaken premise that by doling out dollars they are somehow making a difference. But often they're not. Too many times they're only enabling bad behavior by giving to those who are lazy and unwilling to work. Systems should encourage responsible behavior and build a sense of self-worth.

"We have to address the gaping wounds in our society much more effectively. We have to work to reconcile socio-economic inequities that seize underserved communities. We must provide better education and better opportunities for people to build a better life. We have to focus on prevention more than remediation. We have to break the generational and emotional bonds that keep people enslaved to a system. We must provide spiritual direction and hope. We must equip them to assume personal responsibility for their own future.

And organizations cannot work in isolation. They must become much more collaborative. They must work together to layer and scaffold their services from cradle to grave. Only then can we begin to truly transform society." Dusty was becoming a bit animated, and he recognized it. "OK. That's my soapbox. Now I'll step down for a while," he said, flashing a grin.

"No, please continue. This is good stuff," Joe pleaded. "What's the solution? How do we fix major problems in our society if most of our structures are destined to fail?"

"We have to strategically apply our resources to have the highest impact. We have to find ways to solve the systemic issues that perpetuate the problems. The best organizations are holistic in their approach. They think in terms of *BIG PICTURE*. They share solutions and work to create wrap-around services. In other words, they consciously connect with other groups to have broader impact. Instead of hoarding resources, they look for ways to collaborate and extend their resources. The organizations with this type of focus are those doing the greatest good. And their donor base is emotionally engaged. Their supporters don't just give money, but actually get personally involved in championing the causes that they support. They tend to trade long-distance, short-term mission trips for short-distance, long-term relationships."

16

Value Creation

"Each of us must decide how we are going to steward our time, talents, and treasures," Dusty continued.

Joe thought that was an odd term and wondered what exactly he meant by it, so he asked, "Steward? What do you mean by that?"

"To steward just means to engage wisely. A lot of people work hard to get all they can, can all they get, and then sit on the can! In my opinion, that's not only a waste, but also terribly irresponsible. We are each given certain opportunities and blessings in life. If all we do is hoard them, we've missed the whole point of our purpose on this planet," Dusty said.

"Meaning is found in discovering your gifts. But purpose is found in giving them away. Life is precious and we cannot waste it. Every person is important. We must honor everyone and seek to do good when we can."

Meaning is found in discovering your gifts. But purpose is found in giving them away. Life is precious and we cannot waste it. Every person is important. We must honor everyone and seek to do good when we can.

"You're waxing a bit eloquent there, Dusty," Joe mildly chided with a grin. "But it's all beginning to make sense. I've been thinking about my own life. I've been very fortunate. I've been blessed in so many ways. But I have to confess that even with all of the trappings of success, my life feels a bit hollow. And recently a series of strange events caused me to question my very existence."

"You mean a series of coincidences?" Dusty offered.

"Exactly!" Joe quickly responded. "But now I realize they're not so random after all. For a long time, I think I walked through life with blinders on. Frankly, I didn't care about much other than my own success and happiness.

I was focused on taking care of myself and my family. Not that my intentions were bad. They just left me feeling unfulfilled.

"And to be honest, even with all the success, happiness wasn't what I was experiencing. As a matter of fact, the more success I attained, the more I wanted. And the more I wanted, the less I felt content. Like a hamster on a wheel, I chased something I couldn't have. Does that make any sense, Dusty?"

"It makes perfect sense," Dusty responded. Everyone wants to be happy. The problem is that so few actually experience it. That's because happiness isn't something that can be achieved. It is the byproduct of doing good for others. The more happiness you bring into the lives of others, the more you will experience it yourself. As a husband, I'm happiest when my wife is happy. As a father, I'm happiest when my kids are happy. As a team leader, I'm happiest when my team members are happy. When I do good for others, I feel good!"

> *Everyone wants to be happy. The problem is that so few actually experience it. That's because happiness isn't something that can be achieved. It is the byproduct of doing good for others.*

Joe's mind was reeling. It was as if everything was coming into focus for the very first time. "So where do I start? I mean, where do I jump in to make a difference?"

"I'm encouraged by your enthusiasm," Dusty said, "but before you take a leap, let's talk about another concept first."

"Alright, what's that?" Joe was deeply curious about where this was going.

"Well, in life there are two kinds of people: There are Value Creators and there are Value Extractors. A Value Extractor is someone who comes to the table to get as much for themselves as they possibly can. They live with a 'scarcity mentality.' They believe there isn't enough to go around, so they have to get to the table first and get as much for themselves as they possibly can in order to survive. They take more away than they bring to the table. In essence, they're takers!

Value Creators, on the other hand, have an 'abundance mentality.' They live by the guiding principle that if we all bring more to the table than we take away, at the end of the day there will be a surplus on the table that can be shared by all who helped to create that value. They intentionally look for opportunities to give to others in a way that will benefit everyone involved. They are the givers in the world.

The truth is that we all tend to lean more toward being Value Extractors than we care to admit. We all have a default setting of selfishness. Even when we act like a Value Creator, we sometimes are motivated as a Value Extractor."

"I'm not sure I'm following you," Joe interrupted.

"Well, sometimes we may think we're doing good when, in reality, we aren't really making a difference with our actions."

"Now you've lost me. Explain what you mean," Joe pushed further.

"Remember the whole conversation yesterday about being stopped by a beggar on the street? He's obviously looking for a handout. As he approaches your car, you begin to feel uncomfortable. You momentarily struggle with what to do. You have a few bucks in your pocket, so you hand him some money. Here's my question: Why would you do that? It's not going to solve his problem. It won't get him off the streets. In fact, if you walked the same street tomorrow, you'd likely have the exact same encounter with the same individual. Nothing would have changed for the better. Your paltry attempt to help wasn't full-blown value extraction, but it certainly wasn't value creation either.

"To take it one step further, some people give to avoid involvement. Some people contribute to a cause because they have no interest in getting involved on a more personal level. Some people give for the recognition. There may be all kinds of tainted motives. I'm not suggesting that giving in itself isn't a good thing. It can be. But if your giving keeps you emotionally distant from the problem, or if there is an ulterior motive, then it may be best not to give at all. The best giving is done when you find something you're passionate about. Then add your time and your talent, on top of your treasure, in an attempt to truly make a difference in the world."

"But how do you know when it's the right situation to get involved?" Joe questioned.

"You have to determine what you're personally passionate about. A good way to begin to explore the possibilities is to ask two questions. The first question is, 'What breaks your heart?' And the second question is, 'What makes your heart burn bright?' Or, to ask those two questions differently, 'If you could truly make a difference, what one thing would you like to change in the world? What captures your imagination – something you deeply care about?' When you answer these questions, then you may very well have found your cause and calling. And whatever the cause you choose, make sure that you seek to create as much value for others as you possibly can. That often means looking for ways to change the systemic issues that have created the problem in the first place."

Though Joe was absorbed in the conversation, he needed to get home. He had secured a tee time for an afternoon round of golf and he couldn't be late. He thanked Dusty for his time and asked if they could continue the conversation at a later time. Dusty agreed to do so, and Joe headed off to enjoy the afternoon on the golf course.

17

TEE TIME

The grass was green and the sky was blue when Joe teed it up on the first hole. He looked forward to enjoying this perfect afternoon with his son and daughter. He had invited Kevin to join them to complete their foursome. While not great at golf, Joe enjoyed the sunshine, fresh air, and time with his kids. Kevin joining them for the afternoon was a bonus. Ever since the extraordinary luncheon at the Coincidence Café, Joe had wanted to spend more time with Kevin outside the office.

After a few mulligans and some good-natured ribbing on the first tee, the foursome set off in their golf carts for more fun in the sun. The first nine holes were an adventure, filled with an abundance of slices off the tee box and errant shots from the sand traps. Good conversation punctuated the afternoon as the four talked about various aspects of their lives. Joe appreciated the way Kevin engaged with his two teens, inquiring about their aspirations and plans for the future.

At the turn, they stopped for a sandwich and some drinks before heading to the 10th tee. Waiting on their burgers, Joe brought up his previous conversation with Kevin. It offered Kevin the opportunity to ask Joe's progeny a curious question. "So, if you could solve any world problem, what would it be? I mean, what is an issue that is big enough to capture your imagination and that you feel you could help change for the better?"

The question was rather deep. Joe wondered if either of them would be able to come up with an answer. It certainly wasn't a question he'd asked either of them previously. Without hesitation, his daughter jumped into the fray.

"I went to a conference recently where the topic of human trafficking was brought to my attention. I never realized just how atrocious and widespread the problem is. I've been mulling over how I might be a part of the solution. I'm not quite sure where to start, but the issue has certainly captured my attention."

Then, without any prompting, his son chimed in, "I've been reading about orphans in Haiti and other third-world countries. So many kids have been pushed into the dark recesses of society, abandoned and abused by a system that doesn't serve them well. Did you know that 68 out of 100 third graders in our own country can't read on grade level? How can we expect a generation to function in society if they can't process information effectively? And it's even worse in third-world countries. I'd really like to do something to change that, so I've reached out to a few organizations that are doing something to address the problem," he said.

Joe was impressed, proud, and perplexed. He was impressed with their answers, proud that they both had given such problems their time and attention, and perplexed because he wondered why neither of them had discussed any of that with him. Then it hit him he had never broached such a conversation with either of his kids.

"Those are both great causes," Kevin affirmed. "When I was your age, all I ever thought about was becoming successful. I focused almost exclusively on my career. But now, I'm more interested in doing something significant. I want to find ways in which I can actually change the world for the good.

I've made a good living; now I want to make life good. I want to encourage both of you to pursue a life that leaves a legacy of good. You may do that personally. You may join a philan-

People like to do good business with businesses that do good.

thropic organization, where you can collaborate with others to solve problems. Or you may find yourself in the business world, encouraging your organization to support a worthy cause. After all, people like to do good business with businesses that do good," Kevin said, challenging them both.

The rest of the round, golf became secondary. The conversation about solving world problems was more engaging by far. The four of them bantered back and forth, exploring the subtle nuances of each problem and suggesting ways to address each. They threw out a wide array of creative ideas and debated which possible solutions might be more sustainable. Joe couldn't remember ever having a more meaningful conversation with his children.

Before parting paths in the parking lot, Kevin invited both teens to be his guests at lunch the following Friday at the Coincidence Café. He explained that a group of young people, very much like themselves, would be giving a presentation and fielding questions about a project they were coordinating in South America. Both enthusiastically agreed to attend the lunch meeting. Joe beamed with pride. It was the perfect conclusion to a very poor round of golf.

18

A Bigger Story

The entire week, Joe was filled with anticipation about the luncheon on Friday. He and Kevin met his son and daughter in the parking lot just before noon and they all entered the café together. They headed toward the small meeting room overflowing with attendees. It was so full, in fact, that the buffet lines were set up just outside the room. Kevin introduced Joe's children to two of the leaders from the organization that was presenting. Shortly thereafter, lunch was served. They engaged in small talk as they made their way through the buffet lines. Once everyone had eaten, Hunter again launched the meeting.

"Today we have the privilege of hearing from an impressive team of young people who are committed to changing the world for good." With that brief introduction, Hunter turned the meeting over to a young man who didn't yet look to be in his 30's. He was clean cut and very well-spoken.

"I understand you've been talking recently about the issue of homelessness. It's truly an honor to be with you today because the purpose of our organization is to end global homelessness."

His very first statement was a mic-drop moment. When the young man made that bold declaration of purpose, Joe looked around the room to check the reaction of others. More than a few were smirking with what Joe interpreted as a tinge of skepticism. Joe thought it was a rather audacious statement himself and wondered what kind of strategy they planned to deploy to resolve such a worldwide issue. But Joe also noticed that his kids weren't smirking. In fact, they were already locked in and listening intently.

"A few years ago, I was involved in a service project in Haiti," the young man continued. "I was overwhelmed with the poverty I saw. People living in squalid conditions, without basic necessities of life. Many lived in shanties made from whatever debris they could find. People were barely surviving day to day. Parents with no hope. Kids with no future. It broke my heart. Something had to be done.

"When we returned home, several of us who had been on the trip started dreaming about how we could make a difference. We started a non-profit organization to address the issue. We wanted to create a sustainable and transparent system that might have a broad impact. We sought help. We strategized and applied for start-up accelerator assistance. The response amazed us. People from all walks of life and leaders of other philanthropic organizations began to support the vision. We started off small. In our first six months, we funded the construction of sixteen homes. Not a bad start, but nothing crazy. Then we were challenged by the start-up accelerator to build a hundred homes in a hundred days. Now that was crazy! That summer, we built 113 homes. And things just kept getting crazier! In the next four years, we built 16 transformative communities in Haiti, El Salvador, Bolivia, and Mexico.

"We've had the privilege of partnering with organizations that we could never have imagined. Recently, we combined forces with a group that has the technology to build housing with a 3-D printer—a massive stylus literally pours the concrete walls. Now we can construct in days what would've previously taken months. And we've only just begun. We plan to change the world for good!" he declared, before pausing for questions.

At first, the room fell silent. It was as if everyone was in shock. Then the questions started to flow fast and furiously.

"What's your strategy to accomplish such an ambitious goal?" someone asked.

"We know we can't do it alone, so we're sharing what we've learned. We're sharing everything from our design processes to our technology platform and innovations with other housing organizations. And we're partnering with governments to streamline the process so that, together, we can end survival-mode living for the 1 billion people on the planet who lack housing."

"But why housing specifically?" another inquired.

"Because more people lack safe shelter than any other basic human need. And because homelessness robs people of more than shelter. It takes away a family's security, health, and opportunity to thrive together. Housing provides not only safety, but also better sanitation and the opportunity to focus on other issues. When this basic human need is met, then people can focus on educating their children and growing their income," he responded.

It was a clear and compelling answer. Joe flashed back to his conversation with Kevin about Maslow's *Hierarchy of Need*s. The lowest and most basic tier was *Physiological Needs*. This includes food, shelter, and clothing. Joe remembered that Maslow hypothesized that until these basic needs were met, nothing else really mattered because people would spend their time and energy simply seeking to survive.

"But why are you doing it in other countries when there's an epidemic of homelessness in our own country?" someone else asked.

"That's a great question," the young man acknowledged. "I'm asked that question all the time. The best answer that I can give you is that it provides the most efficient path to higher impact and innovation. First, our dollar goes further in other countries. This quite simply increases speed, decreases costs, and provides quicker proof of concept with less friction. It allows us to move more quickly toward scalability and share-ability. It's easier for us to pioneer solutions where our money goes further and where there is less bureaucracy to navigate. It's a matter of good stewardship. But, at some point, we hope that government agencies will adopt our approach to help stateside too," he stated emphatically.

"How can someone get involved?"

"Well, you can always support us through donations. But our greater desire is to get people involved beyond their checkbook. In addition to your money, we'd be delighted if you would consider giving of your time and experience. We believe that passion is the result of personal involvement. We would welcome you to join us on a project. There, you'd have the opportunity to interact with locals who are helping in the construction of their own communities. When you see firsthand the impact of what's being done, it will change you forever. You might also consider serving on a team of advisors. If you have a specialty, or relational connections with like-minded folks that you think could serve to accelerate our endeavors, we will welcome your input. We want people who truly care about the cause and are committed to making a difference. We're looking for world-changers!" he concluded.

The energy in the room was palpable. The conversation continued for a little longer before the crowd was dismissed. Several people lingered afterward to have additional questions answered. Joe's two teens were right in the middle of the mix, engaged in lively conversations with the presenting team members. Joe and Kevin sat side by side, soaking it all in from across the room.

"You know," Kevin said, "There's a lot of talk these days about the 'Next Gen-ers' being lazy and feeling entitled. But it's certainly refreshing to see these young people living with a deep sense of purpose, and with a passion to change the world!"

Joe smiled and nodded in agreement.

19

LIFE SUPPORT

Joe had been going daily to the hospital to see his father. His condition wasn't improving, so the family made the decision to all go together. It was Sunday afternoon and visitation hours in the CCU were about to end so that the staff could serve the evening meal. The nurse allowed the whole family to enter the room in order to spend time together. Joe's father was on oxygen and struggling to speak. The nurse pulled Joe aside and told him that, given his father's condition, it may not be too long until they would have to put him on life support.

When she exited the room, Joe continued their previous conversation about living in a way so as to leave a legacy. The last few conversations they'd had Joe knew he would cherish forever. The change in his father was overwhelming. To witness how he'd transformed from being a self-focused and driven businessman to contemplating what really mattered in life meant more to Joe than words could express. His father was living proof that seeking what Joe now recognized as *Self-Transcendence*, or giving of yourself to others, was the path to happiness and meaning in life. He had never seen his father so at peace and content, even in his critical condition.

After a while, Joe transitioned the conversation and began sharing about the luncheon at the café. Soon his two teens jumped into the conversation and spoke with enthusiasm about what they had heard. They told their grandfather about their encounters with team members and how they had both gathered information on the organization. They also talked about how they wanted to participate in a trip the team was taking to aid in the construction of a community in El Salvador.

Their grandfather smiled and softly said, "I'm so proud of you both. I wish I'd been challenged at your age to make a real difference with my life. The world is in good hands as long as there are young people like you around." He paused and looked intently at each of them. "If you decide to go on that trip to

El Salvador, I'm paying for it. I want to make that investment in your future. It would give me great joy to do that for you."

They hugged their grandfather and thanked him for his generous offer. Joe somehow knew in his heart that a new legacy was being written. He didn't know exactly what that meant, but he was pretty sure each of their lives had been changed forever.

The family stayed a little longer and exchanged stories, laughter, and tears. Somehow, they each sensed that the end of a life was near. Oddly, sadness was shrouded in the hope of new beginnings. They were writing a new story now. One that was bigger. One that was better. One that was filled with the possibility that they could each contribute to building a brighter tomorrow. Not just for one another, but for others that they may encounter. "Life support" had taken on a whole new meaning.

20

THE JOURNAL

It was early Tuesday morning when Joe received the call that he had expected. His father had passed away peacefully in his sleep. After calling the office to rearrange his schedule, Joe spent the rest of the day coordinating details with the hospital and funeral home.

Later that afternoon he went to the hospital to pick up his father's belongings. Among the articles was a journal. It surprised Joe to find it among his father's possessions. He had never known him to keep a journal. He was curious to see what his father felt was worth documenting. At the same time, he hoped he might find any final wishes his father may have had about his service.

On the way home, he decided to swing by the Coincidence Café to have a cup of coffee and take some time to reflect on all that had happened in recent weeks. As he entered, several team members greeted him and expressed their condolences. Word had certainly spread quickly about his father's passing. Every person who spoke to Joe had something positive to say about their encounters with his father. Their comments genuinely surprised Joe, as he had no idea that his father had frequented the café before his hospitalization.

After placing his order, he took a seat at a quiet table in the back corner—the very same table where he and Sam sat the first time he visited the café. He opened his father's journal and began to read. Minutes turned into hours as he sat there, engrossed in the unfolding story. His father wrote profusely as a man who had many regrets in life. Many of those regrets revolved around not being physically or emotionally present for his family as he built his career. He confessed that he had lived a rather selfish life. He described how he had lost his marriage and had effectively alienated his sons. Joe was reading the written words of a broken man.

But then Joe's father began to recount a series of events that had radically changed his thinking and, subsequently, challenged him to live out his remaining days differently. Joe read about how he had been accosted by a scruffy person who had asked him a haunting question. A question that caused him to reevaluate his entire life. That transformational question was, "Why do you do what you do?" He described in detail the apparently homeless man who had posed the question. Of course, Joe immediately recognized him as being Sam. But he was intrigued by the details of their encounter. The two met just outside the hospital, only moments after Joe's father had received the diagnosis from his doctor. One of the nurses had asked Sam to follow Joe's father outside when she saw how distressed he was. It was no coincidence that Sam had been visiting someone else at the hospital that day. Nor that the nurse knew Sam well and made such a request.

Joe's father was forced to face a painful revelation: Everything he'd worked so hard to acquire meant absolutely nothing in light of the fatal diagnosis. It all seemed for naught. The long hours, the missed ball games, the forgotten birthdays and anniversaries were only a part of the trade-off of climbing the ladder of success. Now he realized the ladder that he'd been climbing led to nowhere. There was nothing on the roof. It was a heart-wrenching reality that his pursuits promised everything but delivered little of real value. At that very moment, Sam asked him the question.

He described how he couldn't even answer. He just broke down and began to cry. "It must have been quite a sight to see," his father wrote in the journal. "There I was sitting on a bench outside the Medical Center in one of my best suits. I was crying like a baby, while being comforted by a homeless man. I can only imagine what people must have thought!"

Tears began to well up in Joe's eyes as he continued to read, "I had nowhere to turn. I was estranged from everyone that I had ever loved. Why did this crazy beggar care enough to listen to my story and cry with me?"

Joe's father recounted the actual conversation that had taken place that fateful afternoon. It was, according to his own words, a divine encounter.

"Your life isn't over yet," the vagabond said. "So what do you want to do with the rest of it?"

"You don't understand. I don't think I have much time left," I said.

"Doesn't really matter! An hour, a day, a month, a hundred years—how do you want to use whatever time is entrusted to you? Do you want to do something significant with the time you have left or do you just want to run out the clock?"

"How can I do something significant when this is a battle I'm not going to win?" I asked. His response hit me like a ton of bricks.

"Perhaps we need to redefine 'win,'" he said. "No one defeats death! Time on earth is limited for everyone. But a win is when you do something good for someone that they couldn't do for themselves. That's how you create a legacy. You can start something good. You can plant a tree, though you may never enjoy its shade. You've made a good living. Now it's time to make life good for someone else. Maybe in giving, you'll find you can start living. And in doing so, you may likely come face to face with the Giver of Life and get caught up in a divine conspiracy of coincidences."

Joe's father continued to put pen to his thoughts: "It was an odd epiphany. To think that I could do some good for someone else brought a ray of hope into my hopeless situation. And the first ones I thought about were my sons. I knew it had to start there. But I had no idea how to reach them. Because of my selfish actions, they had emotionally distanced themselves from me. I couldn't blame them. I had been arrogant and self-absorbed. I had wounded them deeply and I feared they would never be able to find it in their hearts to forgive me.

Over the next few weeks, Sam and I met at the Coincidence Café and an idea evolved. I would seek to find a way to connect with my sons. At the same time, Sam would be on the lookout for a blue Mercedes-Benz EQS 450 sporting a vanity plate that read 'STYLING,' that frequently passed through this area."

In that moment, Joe realized that he'd been targeted! It wasn't serendipitous Sam approached his car that particular day. It wasn't coincidental when he bumped into Sam at the hospital. It was all the most beautiful of set-ups. It had been a conspiracy from the beginning. A divine conspiracy. And he saw their actions for what they truly were—a demonstration of their love.

Joe turned the page. "Contact made. Time to launch a new legacy," his father wrote. Then he listed the contact information of the lawyer responsible for handling his Last Will and Testament. Joe would soon find out that after taking care of those closest to him, his father had left a very sizable portion of his estate to a handful of charitable causes he had grown to appreciate. "My regret," he wrote, "is that I am not able to give more of my time and talent. My treasures will have to do." He also wrote about how he wanted some very specific articles, which held deep sentimental value, to be given to each of his children and grandchildren. And he wrote lengthy personal passages, expressing his dreams and hopes for each of them.

Lastly, he had a list of instructions for his memorial service. The first of his last requests was that Sam preside over the service. He wanted it held at a chapel not too far from where Joe was seated as he read. And the reception afterward was to be held at the Coincidence Café. It all seemed so perfectly fitting.

Joe made the arrangements.

21

A NEW BEGINNING

The crowd that gathered packed out the small chapel for what would prove to be a most memorable memorial service. Though Joe made the arrangements, his father had requested he remain seated with his family for the service. Joe wondered if it was because his father didn't want to put him in the awkward position of struggling to find good things to say. Joe sat between his mother and his wife, Kathy, with their children flanking them. It had taken quite a bit of coercion to get his mother to finally agree to attend. His brother sat in the row behind them, with his own family at his side. The remaining rows were filled with business acquaintances and friends from the old neighborhood. A number of folks that Joe had met at the café attended, but the vast majority of people Joe had never seen before.

A local pastor read the eulogy and two passages from the Bible. Then Susan, a co-owner of the café, sang a song. A leader from a local homeless shelter spoke about how Joe's father had recently been serving meals and assisting men with their job searches. Then the leader of another local charity told a story of how Joe's father had made a significant contribution, at a critical time, that allowed their work in the community to continue. After Susan sang a second song, Sam stepped up to the podium.

Joe had never seen Sam in a suit before. It was completely out of character. His thin frame, wiry hair, and scraggly beard were the same, but now they were dressed up in classy threads.

"I thought I would dress appropriately for the occasion," Sam said to lighten the heavy atmosphere. "I've always been told that the clothes make the man. I never believed it, but that's what I've been told," he said as the crowd chuckled. "This suit was actually given to me by my friend that we are here to honor today. He was wearing it the night I first met him. It fits me perfectly, don't you think?

Shortly after our encounter, he gave it to me because he thought I needed it. I didn't. But I kept it because it was such a kind gesture. A gesture from a kind man who had a good heart.

Although, if he were able to speak to you today, he would tell you that he wasn't always so kind and that his heart wasn't always so good. But that all changed as of late, when life threw him a curveball. You see, until recently, he never thought much about his mortality. He wasn't prepared for life to end. And when you're not prepared for life to end, then you're certainly not prepared to fully live it. Until recently his life had revolved around him. He gave little thought to what he'd done that might last beyond his lifetime. He never pondered eternity or considered his legacy. He never slowed down long enough to smell his own exhaust or analyze the wake he was leaving in the world. But life has a way of teaching us things we're unable or unwilling to learn any other way. Sometimes reality shows up in the most unexpected ways. And when it does, it can turn your life upside down. That's exactly what happened to my friend.

> *When you're not prepared for life to end, then you're certainly not prepared to fully live it.*

With the quickness of a heartbeat, he became sober. It's always sobering when you discover life doesn't revolve around you. For the first time, he was no longer drunk on himself. The withdrawal process was painful as he assessed his life. But the transformation was necessary. And it was glorious. When he reached the end of his own resources, he was left with no other option but to reach to Heaven for help. And he found it. When the scales fell from his eyes, he better understood time and eternity. He began to see the world around him in a new light and started to realize how he could make a difference by helping others. So that's exactly what he did. He didn't squander the opportunity to make a change. Embracing his new reality, he relished every chance to do good. He gave because he'd been given a new life. For the first time, he found clear spiritual direction. Realizing how deeply he had been blessed, he became a blessing to others.

The young woman who just sang for you was one of those touched by his generosity. With very little support, she was working two jobs while attempting to get her degree in music from the local college. She was waiting tables when they met. He asked a few questions and listened intently to her story. Some might describe it as a chance encounter, but I like to think of it as a divine coincidence," Sam smiled at the crowd.

"They were placed on converging paths so that their stories would intersect. And when they did, my friend knew he could help. So he did. Now she's a co-owner of the Coincidence Café and her college tuition is fully funded.

And when my friend was introduced to the work of the homeless shelter, he saw an opportunity to invest some of his time and knowledge, helping those whom many might consider less fortunate. In the process, he discovered he was the greatest beneficiary of his own benevolence. He felt good about doing good. And it became an addiction for him.

He changed from the inside out. After his world changed, he developed a passion to change the world around him. Oh, not the whole world. He knew he couldn't do that. But he was convinced he could change his small corner of it. So he set out to do for one what he wished he could do for everyone. And in doing so he changed the world for someone. In fact, he's changed the world for several someones. Many of you are here today because his life collided with yours in a positive way.

It all started with a simple question: 'Why do you do what you do?' When you can answer the Why question with clarity and conviction, then you may very well have discovered your purpose in life."

With the Why question revealed for all to consider, Sam shifted from storyteller to counselor, making his closing comments more personally pointed.

"So how would you respond to the Why question? The answer must always begin with 'Because.' 'I do what I do Because …!' My friend found his Because. His life and his legacy now challenge each of us to find our own Because. Because is your answer to Why?"

The crowd sat in rapt silence, hanging on Sam's every word. As he closed, he invited everyone to adopt a creed—a manifesto of sorts. A call to action for those who would commit to be world changers. As he closed the service, this is what he read:

Meaning is found in discovering your gift.
Purpose is in giving it away.
Life is precious.
I will not waste it.
Every person, important.
I will honor everyone.

I will live on purpose.

I seek neither fame nor applause.
Accolades will not define who I am.
Making a difference is not an afterthought.
It is my guiding principle.
Ordinary is not my only option.
And, good enough simply isn't.
I defy the drift toward mediocrity.
I will exceed expectations.
I will be intentional with my life.
I will leave a positive wake in the world.

I will live for a purpose.

Life is bigger than me.
I want to leave a mark that is not easily erased.
So, I will...
Give when others take.
Notice what others ignore.
Engage while others walk on by.
Spread kindness.
Inspire hope.

Create value for everyone I encounter.
And encourage others to do the same.

And I will live with purpose.

Everything begins with a choice.
Therefore, every choice is important.
So, I choose...
To be neon in a world of grey.
To be a symphony where formerly there was silence.
To offer my hand as I follow my heart.
To make someone's story better.
To do for one what I wish I could do for everyone.
To rock my world for good.
Today, I choose to be what I was designed to be!
Today, I choose to make a statement with my life!
Today, I choose to be Remarkable!

Sam concluded with a challenge. "Today, and every day that you are given, is the gift of life. You choose how to live it. Choose to be Remarkable!"

It was a poignant conclusion to a glorious celebration of life. A celebration punctuated with a challenge. As the service ended, Hunter offered a final prayer and invited everyone to join the family for a reception at the Coincidence Café.

There, lively conversation and laughter reverberated throughout the humble establishment. Joe heard stories of his father's compassion and kindness that he'd never heard before. For the first time in a long time, Joe was actually proud to be the son of his father. And as Joe watched his own children that afternoon, he couldn't help but wonder what kind of legacy was being born in their hearts.

> *Everyone can make a difference in the world. How will you?*

It seemed appropriate that this particular gathering of family and friends was taking place in the café where it all started, surrounded by those quotes and questions hand-scrawled on the walls. The very same thoughts that had turned his world upside down, but right-side up:

> *Coincidence is just God's way of remaining anonymous.*

"Everyone can make a difference in the world. How will you?" "Everyone has a purpose. What's yours?"

Why do you do what you do?

"Coincidence is just God's way of remaining anonymous."

But the question on the wall that had shaken him to his core and set his life on a new, higher trajectory was, "Why do you do what you do?"

EPILOGUE

Joe's son and daughter went on the trip to El Salvador to help in the construction of a community. The life-altering trip made an indelible impression on them that would not easily be erased. It set their lives on a higher trajectory, igniting a passion to be world-changers.

While they were there, they met an orphan who had bounced around in foster care. The bright young man had dreams of doing great good, but his situation provided little opportunity to bring those dreams to fruition. Upon returning from the trip, the two teens relayed their experience to Joe and Kathy.

Together, they made arrangements to sponsor the young man and bring him to the United States until he completed high school. They also financed his college education. This sacrificial commitment, they agreed, would be a wise use of a portion of the inheritance they had received from Joe's father's estate. And it made Kathy very happy and proud that they could play such a role in changing someone's world. It was part of their own legacy unfolding.

Speaking of legacy, Joe's father's will established a foundation that was specifically dedicated to expanding the footprint and impact of the Coincidence Café concept. Soon multiple locations sprang up all over the city, co-owned by many folks whose lives had been transformed by the generosity of others. Joe was selected as Executive Director of the foundation and Sam was appointed Chairman of the Board. Their commitment was simple: "Change the world for good!"

As for Sam, stories abound and speculation runs rampant. Some say he's an angel sent from Heaven to provide help for those in need. After all, he does always seem to show up at just the right time, in just the right place, with just the right message, for just the right person. Others say he's simply a regular guy with an eccentric flair and a gift for loving people. Those who know him best believe him to be both.

QUESTIONS FOR REFLECTION

Answering the following questions will help you begin to align your gifts, passion, and strengths to find your purpose and make the world a better place. Take time to reflect on each question below and write your answer in the space provided. Remember, your life is a gift to the world. What kind of gift do you want to give?

Q: Before reading *Make Life Good*, how would you have responded if someone were to ask you, "Why do you do what you do?"

A:

Q: What issue makes your heart break?

A:

Q: What issue makes your heart beat fast?

A:

Q: What can you do for one that you wish you could do for everyone?

A:

Q: Who is your someone?

A:

Q. Everyone can make a difference in the world. How will you?

A:

Q: Everyone has a purpose. What's yours?

A:

Q: What legacy do you want to create?

A:

Q: You can plant a tree, even if you never enjoy its shade. When, where, and how do you want to start? What's your next step?

A:

Q: Now, having read *Make Life Good* and pondering these questions, how would you respond if someone were to ask you, "Why do you do what you do?"

A: Because ...

Dr. Randy Ross is a compelling communicator, craftsman of culture, and bestselling author of multiple books, including *Remarkable!*, *Relationomics*, and *Fireproof Happiness*.

Working with brands such as Delta Air Lines, GE Appliances, McDonald's, Panasonic, Cox Communications, Compass Group, Chick-fil-A, Berkshire Hathaway, and the InterContinental Hotels Group, he has inspired and enabled countless people to find new passion and purpose in their work, work better together in teams, and have greater influence and impact.

When people like what they do, they do it better. When people like those they do it with, they work better together. When they like the impact they're having, they find meaning and fulfillment in what they do. Dr. Ross helps them unlock their passion while building healthier relationships and pursuing a purpose beyond self.

As the CEO of Remarkable! and a former Chief People Officer, Dr. Randy Ross utilizes his experience to engage audiences worldwide with his keen insight and contagious humor. He is a messenger of practical wisdom and needed hope, untangling the biggest challenges facing today's business leader, tomorrow's workforce, and the future marketplace. He lives with his wife, LuAnne, and their four children in Atlanta, Georgia.

For more information or speaking requests, visit:
DrRandyRoss.com.

A free ebook edition is available with the purchase of this book.

To claim your free ebook edition:

1. Visit MorganJamesBOGO.com
2. Sign your name CLEARLY in the space
3. Complete the form and submit a photo of the entire copyright page
4. You or your friend can download the ebook to your preferred device

Print & Digital Together Forever.

Snap a photo

Free ebook

Read anywhere

Printed in the USA
CPSIA information can be obtained
at www.ICGtesting.com
JSHW021107290824
69014JS00004B/116

9 781636 983592